Bullies
&
Victims

. . . have patience with everything unresolved in your heart and to try to love the questions themselves as if they were locked rooms or books written in a very foreign language. Don't search for the answers, which could not be given to you now, because you would not be able to live them. And the point is, to live everything. Live the questions now. Perhaps then, someday far in the future, you will gradually, without even noticing it, live your way into the answer.

Rainer Maria Rilke
excerpted from *Letters To A Young Poet*,
as translated by Stephen Mitchell.

Bullies
&
Victims

Helping Your Child Survive the
Schoolyard Battlefield

SuEllen Fried, A.D.T.R.,
and
Paula Fried, Ph.D., Clinical Psychology

M. Evans and Company, Inc.
New York

M. Evans and Company, Inc.
216 East 49th Street
New York, New York 10017

The excerpts in Chapter Seven, Sibling Abuse, are from *SIBLINGS WITHOUT RIVALRY: How to Help Your Children Live Together So You Can Too* by Adele Faber and Elaine Mazlish. Copyright © 1987 by Adele Faber and Elaine Mazlish. Reprinted by permission of the W. W. Norton & Company, Inc.

Library of Congress Cataloging-in-Publication Data
Fried, SuEllen
    Bullies & victims : helping your child through the schoolyard
    battlefield / SuEllen Fried and Paula Fried.
        p. cm.
    ISBN 0–87131–807–5 (cloth)
    1. Bullying—United States. 2. Bullying—United States—Prevention.
3. School violence—United States. I. Fried, Paula.
II. Title.
LB3013.3.F75   1996   96-20589
371.5'8—dc20   CIP

Design and typesetting by Peggy Bloomer, Image Associates

Manufactured in the United States of America

9 8 7 6 5 4 3 2 1

To Kimberly Anne Weisel

Whose brief life touched ours and inspired this book

Contents

Introduction xi

CHAPTER ONE   The Case of Nathan 1

CHAPTER TWO   Understanding the Dimensions of Bullying 5

CHAPTER THREE   Physical Abuse 13

CHAPTER FOUR   Verbal Abuse 31

CHAPTER FIVE   Emotional Abuse 45

CHAPTER SIX   Sexual Abuse 55

CHAPTER SEVEN   Sibling Abuse 16

CHAPTER EIGHT   Bullies and Victims 85

CHAPTER NINE   Empowering Children 107

CHAPTER TEN   Strategies for Adult Intervention 129

CHAPTER ELEVEN   Solutions and Successful Models 151

CHAPTER TWELVE   Challenges for Prevention 173

Appendices 189

Ackowledgments 209

Index 215

Bullies
&
Victims

Introduction

WHEN NATHAN FARIS, a young boy in De Kalb, Missouri, shot a classmate and committed suicide in 1989, it was evidence of a shameful problem that had been long denied. Since then, similar tragedies have been repeated far too many times. As recently as February of 1996, two students and an algebra teacher in Moses Lake, Washington, were killed by a fourteen-year-old honor student, Barry Loukaitas. The incident stunned the school, and the reported speculation was that Loukaitas had been the target of taunts by fellow classmates.

Not everyone holds to the notion that bullying is benign. A number of researchers have been surveying students and collecting data over a period of years. Their results should cause us great alarm.

PARAMETERS OF THE PROBLEM
Consider these statistics:

- American schools harbor approximately 2.1 million bullies and 2.7 million of their victims (Dan Olweus, researcher, journal article of the National School Safety Center).
- 76.8 percent of students in a midwestern study, say they have been bullied and 14 percent of those students indicated that they experienced severe reactions to the abuse (Study conducted by John H. Hoover, Ronald Oliver and Richard J. Hazler).

- The National School Safety Center estimates that 525,000 "attacks, shakedowns and robberies" occur in an average month in public secondary schools.
- It is estimated that 160,000 children miss school every day, due to fear of attack or intimidation by other students. (National Education Association).
- A survey conducted by the American Association of University Women reported that 85 percent of girls and 76 percent of boys have been sexually harassed in some form and only 18 percent of those incidents were perpetrated by an adult.
- Young bullies carry a one-in-four chance of having a criminal record by age 30 (study by Leonard Eron and Rowell Huesmann).
- The National Education Association reports that every day, 6,250 teachers are threatened with bodily injury and 260 are physically assaulted.

Despite these frightening statistics, the issue of bullying has been largely ignored as a serious social problem. We believe there are several reasons why:

1. Bullying is so widespread and so common that the "rite of passage" myth has blinded us to its extensive harm.
2. Because bullying involves children, it is seen as a minor issue on the horizon of adult crises.
3. Since children are viewed as powerless in our society, adults are often oblivious to the insidious power structure that is a part of bullying.
4. Experience tells us that the prevalence of a problem does not bring about change until concerned citizens take action.

5. There is a history of abuse denial in our society that has prevented us from acknowledging child, spouse, and elder abuse.

A BRIEF HISTORY

Infanticide has been a common practice in many cultures. Children, as well as wives, have been viewed as the property of the head of the household.

The role of child as an obedient servant without rights was not questioned in America until the case of Mary Ellen McCormack came to light in 1874. At the age of ten she was discovered in ragged clothes, beaten almost daily, imprisoned in an apartment, and allowed outside only at night. The women who discovered her tried in vain to remove the young girl from her family. In desperation they turned to the American Society for the Prevention of Cruelty to Animals (ASPCA), an organization founded in 1868 to rescue helpless and abused animals from their cruel owners. Because there were no laws to protect children at that time, Mary Ellen was tried as a member of the animal kingdom, under ASPCA legislation. Within twenty-four hours Mary Ellen was removed from the home. The case was taken to trial and she was committed to an orphanage. Consequently, interest in children's rights was briefly heightened but it faded and ultimately dissipated during the Great Depression. In 1960, Dr. C. Henry Kempe coined the term "the battered child" and subsequently presented a paper at the annual meeting of the American Academy of Pediatrics. Over the next ten years, states all across the country created laws to mandate and collect reports of child abuse. The Child Abuse Prevention and Treatment Act was passed by Congress in 1973.

Unfortunately, the public at large was for the most part unaware or unconcerned, even though reports of abuse and neglect of 2,000,000 children were known. An average of three children were being killed every day. It wasn't until 1987 when the story of Lisa Steinberg made headlines that public interest was really captured. Lisa was killed by her father, a successful attorney, while her mother, a professional woman and children's book editor, watched. She waited too long to call for medical help to save her child. How shameful that this story caused more reaction than the appalling statistics that had been reported over such a long period of time!

The term "peer abuse" has not even entered popular vocabulary. How many youngsters will be permanently affected by the actions of other children while we wait for some celebrity tragedy to stir our passion?

Can Bullying Ever Be Eradicated?

We recognize that aggression is an innate human response and that teasing, taunting, and bullying will always be with us in some form or another. We do not expect to eliminate aggression, but we do intend to put some limits on it where children's interaction and well-being is concerned. Just as there are physical signs that roughhousing or punishment has gone too far, such as bruises and cuts, we must learn to recognize the emotional evidence that indicates when a child's safety zone has been violated.

Dan Olweus, one of the earliest researchers in this field, surveyed 150,000 Norwegian students in the 1970s. After determining that bullying was a considerable problem, a nationwide campaign was undertaken in Norwegian comprehensive schools (grades 1-9). In an article published by *The Education Digest*, March 1988, Olweus wrote that statistical analyses indicated that the frequency of bullying problems in forty-two schools in Bergen, Norway, decreased by 50 percent or more in the two years following the campaign. In addition, antisocial behavior in general, such as theft, vandalism, and truancy showed a marked drop during those years. Finally, student satisfaction with school life increased at the same time.

There is every reason to believe that this problem could attract the concern of people in this country. The purpose of this book is to encourage children and adults in partnership to mobilize and put the prevention of bullying on our national agenda. If we fail, cruelty will continue to be condoned and millions of children will suffer.

ABOUT THE AUTHORS

I, SuEllen Fried, am a child advocate and past president of the National Committee to Prevent Child Abuse. My daughter, Paula Fried, is a clinical psychologist in private practice. In the past twenty years Paula and I have taken different paths on a similar journey—a journey that prods us to make people aware of their profound impact on each other, to help them untangle their conflicts and power struggles, and to assist them to achieve more loving, secure relationships.

My time has been spent as a community activist, concentrating on child-abuse prevention. In 1976, I founded the model chapter for the National Committee to Prevent Child Abuse (NCPCA) in Kansas and then became president of the NCPCA in 1980. I am still involved with local, state, and national efforts to prevent family and interpersonal violence. Professionally, I am a dance therapist, using movement as a way to help troubled children, adolescents, and adults express and resolve their conflicts.

Since Paula received her doctorate in clinical psychology she has been working as a psychotherapist with families, adolescents, and children. Her counseling and assessment experience, as well as her research background, give her an important perspective. The purpose of this book is threefold:

- To alert adults and children to the difference between normal peer teasing and bullying situations;
- To help parents, teachers, and counselors under-

stand the dynamics and act effectively when children are bullying or being bullied;

- To empower children to prevent and solve the problem.

CHAPTER ONE

The Case of Nathan

"Bullying is an issue whose time has come."

KIM'S STORY

Kim was a soft-eyed, shy, freckled, nine-year-old girl who was sitting on our patio, wearing a small wig that hugged and hid her bald head. Chemotherapy had caused all of her hair to fall out and she had spent her summer vacation receiving painful bone marrow transplants, chemotherapy, and radiation. When Paula was a freshman in college, she worked that summer as a volunteer in a pediatric oncology unit where Kim had been a patient and they had become friends.

At this farewell luncheon, I met Kim and her mother for the first time. We shared a delightful afternoon and I came to understand why Paula was so fond of this charming young girl. As we began our good-byes, Paula asked Kim if she was looking forward to resuming school. "Oh, yes!" Kim replied. "I've really missed my friends and I can't wait to see them again." Then Paula inquired if Kim had any concerns. She thought for a moment and I wondered if she would speak about the grief work she had been doing. Kim knew that the medical treatments she had endured would only postpone her death, not prevent it. Kim's response to Paula's question launched this book, though we didn't know it at the time. Kim confided that her greatest concern was recess. Recess meant boys knocking off her wig, and teasing her about being bald.

I turned away to conceal my angry tears. Why should a young girl engaged in letting go of her life, her family, her friends, have to endure the jeers of cruel, thoughtless classmates? Kim seemed resigned to her lot. We found it unbearable.

In 1989 an article appeared in the newspaper about a student, victimized by teasing, who shot a classmate and then committed suicide. Another article reported that a student in a junior high school had brought a shotgun to school and killed his principal. His act, too, was the consequence of teasing. We kept coming back to these three incidents as we tried to understand where to draw the line between teasing, bullying, and abuse.

Some teasing is inevitable and can be important preparation for life. The experience of being teased introduces the tension of power struggles, which are an unavoidable part of relationships. Teasing can help us develop a sense of humor, instruct us to be able to laugh at ourselves, and teach us to avoid taking ourselves too seriously. We learn how to "take it" and to hold on to who we really are when others attempt to shred our persona. Teasing can be a form of affection—a communication style that livens family and interpersonal dialogue. Teasing may also be a way that friends "toughen" each other up, an adolescent initiation rite.

At the same time, we know that there is a point when teasing ceases to be helpful or playful, when it becomes humiliating and emotionally abusive, and when the victim requires protection from the teaser. Should teasing be determined by the teaser or by the person who is being teased? What about those who tease with evil intent, knowing full well that their victim is wounded, but claim that "I was only teasing"? Such protests cannot be tolerated as an excuse for cruelty.

If a certain level of teasing is inevitable, then at least we must help children deal with it more confidently.

Our first task is to raise the child's awareness of when he or she is being bullied. Often, children view teasing as an inescapable hazard of their environment, especially when it is not identified by adults as a problem. Even when their suffering increases, children do not always perceive teasing as significant. As a behavior, it can be likened to the tale of a frog who jumped into a pot of boiling water and jumped right out when he became aware of his predicament. Another frog, placed in a pot of cold water, sensed no danger as the temperature gradually increased. By the time the water came to a boil, the poor frog was cooked. Likewise, children who are being teased, may not sense when the level of cruelty is being turned up, and can find themselves in "hot water" before they realize their plight.

This leads us to the case of Nathan Faris. Nathan was an outstanding student. In fact, he was one of the brightest children in his class. Nathan was also overweight. Either of these factors would make him a ripe target for teasing. The combination sealed his fate.

During his elementary school years, Nathan endured endless namecalling, teasing, humiliation, and isolation. As he approached junior high school he hoped that children would be more mature and less cruel. Instead, he found that middle school was even more brutal. Not only did the taunting continue, it increased.

One day Nathan came to school with a gun, shot a fellow student, and then committed suicide in the presence of his classmates.

When did teasing turn into bullying? Is bullying in the same category as abuse? Why did Nathan react so violently? Is the level of bullying that we are seeing today more serious than it was in times past? Is Nathan's reaction a rare exception or is it a more common problem than we have acknowledged?

While we will never know the full story of the fatal shooting in Nathan's classroom, his tragedy raises a host of complicated and confusing issues:

Was it the cruelty of the words or the emotional isolation that led to Nathan's despair . . . or both?

Was his intent to do away with his tormentors or was he trying to punish a classroom of witnesses who had never come to his defense?

Was Nathan dealing with undetected physiological and emotional problems?

What role did Nathan's parents play? Were they aware? Did they ignore his distress or did they try to intervene in some way?

What role did the school system play? Was Nathan's situation ever recognized as psychological terrorism or was it dismissed as harmless teasing?

What was the neighborhood context? How did problems get solved in the community culture?

Was his behavior prompted by influences in the media?

Why does our society regard the cruelty perpetrated against children by other children as less harmful than cruelty committed by adults? Why do we think that harassment or assault between children is less worthy of concern than harassment or assault between adults? As we explore these issues, we hope this book not only will inform you, but also motivate you to put that knowledge into action.

CHAPTER TWO

Understanding the Dimensions of Bullying

"I'm not a bully, I was only teasing!"

LET US BEGIN with a definition of bullying that will help us clarify the difference between harmless and harmful behavior. In an article entitled "Overcoming Bullying Behavior" by Ellen R. Clore, R.N., and Judith A. Hibel, R.N., bullying is described as "one or more individuals inflicting physical, verbal, or emotional abuse on another—includes threat of bodily harm, weapon possession, extortion, civil rights violation, assault and battery, gang activity, attempted murder, and murder." We believe the category of sexual harassment should be added to the definition in light of the number of incidents currently reported.

Whenever we use the term bullying, we are defining it as abuse.

In this chapter, we will clarify the difference between harmless and harmful, or abusive, behavior. Researchers tend to use extreme behaviors to define bullies and victims, and we certainly have extreme examples to share in this book. There are many young people, however, who may not meet the research criteria but, nonetheless, are miserable. If children say they are hurting, isn't that enough? How can we give voice to the valid feelings of those children who may not qualify as victims on a research scale? At the very least we must bring children and adults to the table to begin the dialogue around these issues. Once a critical mass of our society engages in the discussion, perhaps we can rewrite the current script.

Bullying involves both males and females and it can begin at an early age. Pre-school teachers with whom we have spoken acknowledge that the problem is evident with two- and three year olds. These early patterns of behavior tend to remain constant and escalate rather than recede as the child gets older. Aggressive behaviors at an early age can indicate risk for adult criminal behavior. At least 50 percent of children identified as aggressive and conduct-disordered face serious difficulties as adults. One study indicates that young bullies carry a one-in-four chance of having a criminal record by age thirty, as compared with a normally behaved child's chance of one-in-twenty. We will look at the characteristics of these young bullies in a later chapter.

BULLYING: A COMPLEX PROBLEM

The concept of a clear delineation between harmless and harmful teasing might lull us into visualizing this problem as a horizontal band with a line down the center—normal teasing on one side and bullying on the other. We believe the problem is too complicated to be described in such a simplified way. The child who bullies others is affected by a number of factors, best pictured as five concentric circles. Each circle represents a significant element, beginning with the individual child viewed in the context of family, school, community, and culture. We will also examine the consequences of bullying for victims, perpetrators, witnesses, and society as a whole.

The complex factors affecting bullying

The innermost circle consists of the specific personality traits of the individual child (e.g., shyness, assertiveness, poor or good self-esteem), physical characteristics (e.g., height, weight, attractiveness, a specific physical disability), and behaviors (e.g., aggressiveness, passivity, immaturity). Each of these qualities will influence a child's interactions with others. Some children have positive attributes that will be helpful in their relationships, while other children have negative traits and behaviors that make forming relationships more difficult.

The next circle is the family context in which the child lives. Families differ in the number of parents in the home (e.g., one parent, two parents, no parents); and in the style of parenting used (e.g., authoritarian, rigid, flexible, abusive, negligent). Families vary in the amount of emotional support the members provide for each other, and in the level of conflict and tension in the home (this would include the parents' own experience with abuse when they were growing up). Some families falter under the pressure of unemployment, chronic illness, or alcohol abuse, while other families are relatively free of such burdens. These and other differences among families are powerful influences that carry over into a child's relationship with peers.

The school environment provides the next sphere of influence on the child. It includes the teachers' and administrators' ability to handle their own aggressive feelings, the disciplinary philosophy of the school staff, the willingness of the staff to intervene in student conflicts, class size, and the teacher-to-student ratio. These variables in combination help to create a school climate that either discourages or promotes violence.

The next set of factors to consider are found in the specific community in which the child, family, and school are located. Community can refer to a borough; a neighborhood; a scout troop; a Boys or Girls Club; a church, synagogue, or mosque. Other factors that affect the child on this level include the economic level of the community, whether the area is rural or urban, the extent of ethnic diversification, and, in many cases, the quality of social-service agencies. Community attitudes can have great bearing on what kind of interpersonal relationships are considered acceptable or normal.

The final circle is the larger culture that envelops the child, family, school, and community. Important factors include the cultural attitudes toward violence (e.g., violence is exciting, stimulating), cynicism or hopefulness about our ability to solve problems, racism, sexism, and the role of the media in shaping the values of the culture (e.g., the recommended way to resolve conflicts is through use of violence). Cultural contexts exert profound influence.

Throughout our discussion we will consider peer violence from this broad perspective. We see the individual, the family, the school, the community, and the culture as interdependent systems, much like a kaleidoscope. When one piece shifts, the entire pattern is affected. As we describe the problem of bullying, explore the dynamics of abusive relationships, and describe programs and strategies that are being developed to alleviate abuse, we will return to the concentric circle concepts.

Most of the literature on bullying focuses on information collected from children, but, as I traveled around the country speaking about child peer abuse, I was continually moved by stories by adults in the audience, stories revealing scars from childhood taunting and teasing that had occurred decades earlier. Wanting to learn more about adults' recollection of childhood bullying, Paula and I conducted a survey of colleagues around the country who are members of the American Dance Therapy Association. We targeted people working in a helping profession who would be willing to disclose childhood experiences to help us gain insight into the lasting effects of abuse. The survey is included in the back of the book, Attachment A.

Eighty-seven people responded and, from their reports, we learned that 82 percent feel they experienced harmful abuse during their childhood. When asked to characterize the difference between non-harmful teasing and harmful teasing, 5 percent stated that all teasing is harmful and did not see a difference. Those who did pinpointed six factors in defining harmful abuse.

1. **Intent to harm**—the perpetrator finds pleasure in the taunting and continues even when the victim's distress is obvious.
2. **Intensity and duration**—the teasing continues over a long period of time and the degree of taunting is damaging to the self-esteem of the victim.
3. **Power of the abuser**—the abuser maintains power because of age, strength, size, and/or gender,

4. **Vulnerability of the victim**—the victim is more sensitive to teasing, cannot adequately defend him or herself, and has physical or psychological qualities that make him or her more prone to vulnerability.

5. **Lack of support**—the victim feels isolated and exposed. Often, the victim is afraid to report the abuse for fear of retaliation.

6. **Consequences**—the damage to self-concept is long lasting, and the impact on the victim leads to behavior marked by either withdrawal or aggression.

Other results of the survey showed that 70 percent of the respondents described the abuse as verbal (name-calling, teasing, humiliating); 50 percent described the abuse as emotional, (rejecting, isolating, and terrorizing); and 31 percent described the abuse as physical (punching, poking, and beating). Many reported being victims of more than one form of abuse. Males identified only males as perpetrators. Females reported both male and female perpetrators but were more often abused by males.

The respondents indicated that most abuse occurred between the ages of nine and thirteen, when they were in the upper elementary grades and middle or junior high school. Fifty-four percent claimed that they received no support from adults or peers. Of those who felt they had an advocate, 37 percent received support from parents, 22 percent from mothers, 11 percent from siblings, and 11 percent from peers. Only 1 percent said they received support from either teachers or fathers.

The memories were indelible, even though the incidents had taken place many years earlier. Some of the reports were quite poignant. "I was teased verbally during one whole school year by a boy in class because I wore a back brace." "In high school a disabled boy was mocked and jeered at by his peers. I was too far away to do anything and too fearful to get closer." "I still remember being followed home from school by a male peer and harassed for 'killing Christ.' " "As I attempt to answer this survey I remember more and more events from my childhood. Two had long-lasting effects on me. After a boy made fun of how I changed key when I sang, I did not sing alone in anyone's hearing for twenty years. The same boy made fun of how I played baseball (like a ballerina) and I stopped playing sports." A number of respondents reported being teased for being too smart; having a certain religious, racial, or ethnic background; or wearing clothing that was not in fashion. Being overweight was a prime factor for abuse. Other physical qualities that provoked teasing were stuttering, foreign accents, size, and poor athletic ability.

One respondent, an epileptic, could still recall being called crazy because of her *grand mal* seizures. "I remember just coming out of a seizure. I was woozy and unaware. I remember the children standing in a circle about me staring at the urine stain on my clothes. Their look of pity, disgust, horror, and revulsion was hard to swallow. After that they never played with me on the playground and wouldn't choose me for sports."

Examples of sibling abuse were mentioned many times. We also learned that a number of vivid memories were sexual in nature. Females reported incidents of how "a boy tried to pull my pants down," "I was teased because I was the first one to wear a bra," "a boy sat on me and jiggled my breasts," "a girl made me fondle her brother's penis."

Our respondents were equally truthful about the way they treated others. When the question "Looking back, did you ever treat another child or children in a way that was harmful?" was asked, 42 percent acknowledged that they had participated in abuse themselves.

What impressed us most was the depth of feeling still present in the memories of people who took the time to recount their histories. They wrote in great detail, recapturing intense events that took place even forty or fifty years ago.

In spite of the myriad of causes and contributing factors, we are convinced that our best hope for decreasing social violence lies in the prevention of bullying behavior, particularly at the elementary school level. Our children also need to be taught compassion, empathy, respect, and responsibility. Other valuable skills to be taught are assertiveness, anger management, conflict resolution, problem solving, and appreciation of differences. If these important concepts become rooted in children's attitudes when they are young, perhaps we can spare them some of those emotional scars that never quite heal. We might even prevent some of the disastrous situations that erupt from early behavioral patterns.

In summary, bullying includes physical, verbal, emotional, and sexual abuse, involving both males and females. Early patterns of behavior tend to remain constant and they tend to escalate in degree rather than recede. Many adults who felt they were bullied in their youth carry the memories of those experiences for many years. Aggressive behavior at an early age indicates a high risk for adult criminal behavior.

All teasing is not bullying and there are a number of factors that help determine the difference:

- An intent to harm by the perpetrator
- Intensity and duration
- Abuse of power
- Vulnerability of the victim
- Isolation and lack of support for the victim
- Consequences and behavior change for the victim

We believe that bullies and victims should be seen from the perspective of individual, family, school, community, and cultural influences. Both a bully and victim can be struggling with genetic and personality disorders, living in a dysfunctional home environment, causing or experiencing chaos in a school that sets no boundaries or consequences, and being affected by and contributing to a community and culture of callousness.

In the next four chapters we will take an in-depth look at physical, verbal, emotional, and sexual bullying.

CHAPTER THREE

Physical Abuse

"Boys will be boys."

HOW MANY TIMES have you heard that expression? It's amazing how often a catch phrase like that can be used to justify cruelty. In this chapter we will focus on physical bullying/abuse, which includes punching, poking, strangling, suffocating, bending fingers back, burning, poisoning, hair pulling, excessive tickling, biting, stabbing, shooting. One student even reported being held down while cigarette smoke was blown in her mouth until she vomited.

Aaron was minding his own business, marching in a line from music class back to his fifth-grade classroom when Stuart started poking him in the back. Aaron spun around and said "Quit it!" but Stuart continued the poking. Aaron then threatened Stuart and promised to punch him if he didn't stop. Stuart doubted that Aaron would really hit him. Besides, he was bored and Aaron's back was just too tempting. Aaron got angry and pushed Stuart against Maynard. Maynard hit Stuart and Stuart yelled that it wasn't his fault. The three boys got into a shoving match until they had to catch up with the rest of their classmates who had arrived at their classroom. This is an example of the kind of physical interplay that occurs in schools every day—a fairly typical "boys will be boys" incident.

We would not consider this bullying for several reasons. It was a spontaneous interaction, lacking intensity and duration, between children of fairly equal power. There was no real intent to harm and none of the children was hurt, physically, or emotionally.

Stories of icy snowball attacks, braids yanked, and being locked in a closet, which linger in the minds of many adults we've interviewed, are harder to classify. To the people who shared them with us, the actions were considered to be abuse. However, other children have suffered those same outrages without feeling abused.

The next example is more severe, one that we would definitely define as bullying, yet to the teachers it was another case of "boys will be boys." Carl's family moved to a different neighborhood when Carl entered seventh grade. He was a little anxious about entering a new school but he had been fairly popular in elementary school and figured he would be able to fit in at the new junior high. He hadn't counted on being singled out by three athletes who made it a game to pick a fight with him every day. It started in gym class and spread to the halls, for no reason other than that he was the "new kid." Carl had to always be on guard. For two years, Carl fought every day, not because he wanted to but because he had to defend himself. His teachers were aware of the bullying but they never interfered. One time when the whole gym class joined in and he was clearly outnumbered a teacher did step in but Carl was the only one punished. He remembers, clearly, mopping the locker room floors for a week while no consequences were assigned to his assailants. In the summer of his eighth-grade year he made a plan to put an end to the bullying and rancor that had consumed him for two years. On the first day of school in ninth grade, he approached each of his three tormentors separately and told them he was going to forgive them for all the brutality they had inflicted on him and he asked their forgiveness in return for the bitterness he had harbored. They were absolutely stunned and never bothered him again. Carl said that even though he was stuck in a two-year "pity party," he felt there were a lot of other kids in school who endured much worse abuse than he.

A more extreme case is the story of the junior high school student many years ago whose anguish received no attention until a fatal shooting occurred.

Zachary was a young man who became a target for bullying because of his weak physical stature and quick temper. Zack had been dubbed a nerd by his peers and that desensitizing label gave them liberty to pursue him mercilessly. It was no secret that several boys would gang up on him just for the fun of it, while other students encouraged the bullies.

The victim received no support from any of his classmates and in frustration he turned to his parents. His father urged him to fight back, but Zack was not a jock and certainly not physically capable of defending himself against several large boys. He couldn't make his father understand how helpless he was.

His mother was more sympathetic. She went to school on a number of occasions to talk to teachers and the principal but nothing changed as a result. As Zack's frustration increased, he flew into a rage at the slightest provocation. Students enjoyed provoking him and he reliably exploded to meet their expectations. There were other signs that his emotions were out of control, but in those days such matters were not taken seriously. No one involved would have predicted that such "typical" junior high manifestations would lead the young man to take one of his father's guns and turn it on the principal. The possibility was so unfathomable that one teacher who saw Zack walk into the school with the rifle thought he was bringing it to school as part of a speech assignment. It was not uncommon for students to bring war relics for class discussions. It was several years before the building, damaged by sprayed bullets, was completely restored but it probably took much longer to repair the psyches of the students and teachers who will never forget that day.

One lesson this tragedy teaches is to rethink our perception of so-called "normal" teasing and bullying. We cannot accurately predict the breaking point of a beleaguered child and we must relinquish the denial that accompanies sayings like "boys will be boys."

In another high school, thousands of miles away and many years later, we find another example.

Kevin was a junior, editor of the school newspaper, captain of the swimming team, and academically successful. One afternoon, as Kevin opened his locker and started to put on a starter jacket, he was attacked from behind. Kevin was quite tall and, as the assault began, he whirled around to defend himself. He saw that four males were involved. Two were in the lookout position, while the other two students began throwing rocks at his head. Within seconds, he collapsed. As he lay on the ground his assailants kicked him and made off with his prized jacket. He lay there unconscious until some students discovered him and reported the situation to a school administrator.

An ambulance was called and Kevin was rushed to a hospital where his mother was notified that her son was in a coma. Doctors were concerned about possible paralysis. Fortunately, the paralysis was a temporary condition and Kevin ultimately regained consciousness. After spending several anxious days nursing her son through his recovery, Kevin's mother contacted the school principal to discuss the incident.

She was shocked by his response. She reports that he stated that, because it was only a couple of weeks until the end of school, pranks were to be expected. At the close of school each year there was always some caper or escapade for "as we all know, boys will be boys."

These stories illustrate a cavalier attitude that is not uncommon towards young perpetrators of physical abuse. Zack's victimization continued over a long period of time. Kevin was attacked on one occasion. Zack was a class scapegoat. Kevin was a strong, much admired student who had not been previously victimized. Authorities at Zack's school were aware of the constant abuse. The administrators at Kevin's school had no forewarning.

Though different in many respects, these two examples of serious, abusive behavior exemplify the hands-off approach that many schools have adopted.

The incidence of violence and aggression committed by youth has increased dramatically in the past twenty years, beginning with a noticeable rise in the early 1970s. In 1975 the Bayh Senatorial Subcommittee published a survey of 750 school districts in the United States. This survey, called the Safe School Report, indicated that between 1970 and 1973 homicides increased by 18.5 percent, rapes and attempted rapes by 40.1 percent, and the number of weapons confiscated by school personnel by 54.4 percent. Despite the results of the report, there was no national response. Subsequent decades have seen continued increase in violence and aggression among youth.

Statistics collected by the Federal Bureau of Investigation show that one in six arrests for murder, rape, robbery, or assault is of a suspect under eighteen. Slayings by teenagers alone rose by 124 percent between 1986 and 1991. In 1992 young people killed 3,400 people nationwide.

The motives vary. Some are premeditated, some are accidental, some are related to gang initiations, some are impulsive, some seek revenge, some stem from jealousy, some seem to defy explanation.

The following excerpts were reported in newspapers during several months in 1993.

Four children suffered minor injuries Wednesday when their school bus was bombarded with rocks and bottles by a group of children.

A seventeen-year-old suburban youth has been charged with stabbing another teenager in the neck in a fight outside of a convenience store. The victim, also seventeen, suffered a five-inch gash on the left side of his neck that narrowly missed his jugular vein.

Three teenagers will be tried as adults in the bludgeoning deaths of three eight-year-old boys. An autopsy showed they died from head blows. Police haven't given a motive for their deaths, but rumors persist the three were sexually mutilated.

A young boy in Miami was stabbed repeatedly because he inadvertently stepped on a girl's shoe as they boarded a school bus.

A diminutive, thirteen-year-old, friendly, helpful boy who loved to ride his bike and played drums in the grade-school band bludgeoned a four-year-old child to death. He shoveled driveways and took people's garbage out for them. The District Attorney has read the boy's confession but he doesn't know why the killing occurred. "I suspect that when this case is all over, you're going to be asking the same question: Why?" he said.

A two-year-old child was found strangled by a fourteen-year-old male. The murder occurred while the mother of the teenager was babysitting with the young victim.

A fifteen-year-old boy was charged with attempted murder in the shooting of a girl in a crowded high school cafeteria. The victim, who was shot in the head, was in serious condition. The boy and a second youth allegedly were arguing in the cafeteria of their high school when the boy fired the gun. The bullet struck the victim, who was an innocent bystander, according to the authorities.

A December 7, 1995, edition of *USA Today* reported a national poll of young people that found a pervasive fear of violence and early death among children ages seven to ten and widespread experience of crime and violence among teens.

The telephone survey of 1,000 eleven- to seventeen-year-olds (margin of error 3 percentage points), and in-person interviews with 120 seven- to ten-year-olds found that 71 percent of children ages seven to ten worry they might get shot or stabbed at school or home and 40 percent of girls ages fourteen to seventeen know someone their age who has been hit or beaten by a boyfriend.

Each time I speak to a high school class I hear stories about girls who are slapped, punched, beaten, or tickled to the point of pain by their boyfriend. The pairing pressure keeps a lot of young women in physically abusive situations. Jealousy is a reason for many of the attacks. At first, the girls are flattered and see violence as proof of love but ultimately the abuse is more an expression of control than affection. Young men and women who have grown up in violent homes are at risk of repeating the patterns of aggressor/victim they have seen.

The increase in aggression among youth has a new and deadly twist—the ready availability of handguns. Criminologists are convinced that a major factor in the rise in slayings by juveniles is the increased use of guns today as compared to the use of knives in the past.

Jay Winsten, Associate Dean and Director of the Center for Health Communication at the Harvard School of Public Health, Boston, Massachusetts, recalls days past when some slight would propel two boys into a "slugfest." Now the least misstep can provoke a shooting. "Yesterday's fist fight has become today's shootout," says Winsten. "Yesteryear's black eye and injured pride is today's gaping two-inch exit wound with internal injuries."

The prevalence of firearms adds a new dimension to the terror of bullying. In 1987, more than 400,000 students carried handguns to school, including 135,000 who did so daily, according to the Center to Prevent Handgun Violence. Statistics come from a variety of sources, and, although estimates vary slightly, all point to a frightening trend. A survey released by the Louis Harris Research firm in 1993 says that 59 percent of school children in sixth through twelfth grade say they "could get a handgun if they wanted one." More than a third say they could get one "within an hour."

Contrary to the popular perception, the new data shows that handgun violence is not just a problem of inner city children. "It is evident that no part of the country, no area-cities, suburbs, small towns—is immune from the influence of guns among young people today," Harris says. "Higher numbers in the non-public schools say they can get guns than is the case among those who go to the public school."

The National Education Association reports that every school day 160,000 students skip classes because they fear physical harm and forty are killed or hurt by firearms.

Thirty-five percent of the students polled believe their lives will be cut short because of guns. Violence attributed to handguns will cause more adolescent deaths than illness. According to the National Center for Health Statistics, homicide by firearms is now the second-leading cause of death (after motor vehicle crashes) for fifteen- to nineteen-year-old caucasians. For African-Americans in that age bracket, homicide is the leading cause of death. The Education Digest reports that one in twenty high school students carry a gun, and that the number of youth ages fifteen to nineteen who were killed by firearms increased 43 percent from 1984 to 1988. For African-American males in the same age group the increase was over 100 percent during the same period. Fights over girls, sneakers, and sports-related jackets can end in fatal shootings.

"Adolescence is a crazy time, a purgatory between childhood and adulthood," says Neil Blumberg, M.D., a forensic psychiatrist in Baltimore. "When we add handguns to this tempestuous period, we really have an explosive situation."

A dramatic example is the case of Thurman. Thurman was a basketball star at his high school. He was a good student and had dreams of a college basketball scholarship. A rivalry developed with a fellow player, mostly incited by other students who enjoyed pitting the athletes against each other.

Two weeks before high school graduation, an incident occurred on the bus after school. Words were exchanged as Thurman boarded the bus and continued when he reached his stop. He suggested that his rival get off the bus and settle the matter with fists. Thurman was not aware that his competitor was carrying a gun and as he prepared to pull a punch, he was shot in the neck. Thurman is now a paraplegic, his mobility connected to a wheelchair. Fortunately, this remarkable young man is still pursuing his goals. He graduated from college and is enrolled in law school. He spends most of his spare time speaking to students, hoping to prevent a similar incident in their lives.

While homicide rates are decreasing across the country, youth violence is on the rise. Even more disturbing is the age factor. In early 1996, the community of Richmond, California was stunned by the savage beating of a one-month-old infant. The perpetrator was a six-year-old boy!

Bullying is not limited to boys. While males are more frequently identified as bullies, girls are both perpetrators and victims. As perpetrators, girls are more likely to engage in verbal and emotional bullying, rather than physical or sexual harassment, but they are not exempt from such behavior. A recent example occurred in a suburban high school cafeteria. According to a student at the school, one girl asked another a question and felt "dissed" (disrespected) by the response, so she grabbed her by the hair and used an Exacto knife to cut her throat. The wound required twenty-six stitches.

Seven times as many boys as girls say they've shot at somebody, and more than three times as many boys as girls say that someone has shot at them. One study quoted interviews in which several girls said that when they retaliated against their female attackers, the bullying often stopped. For boys, the situation is not as easily solved. Many male students believe that the only solution is to fight violence with violence, or to at least threaten the bully. But retaliation often escalates the cycle of revenge. On the other hand, boys who don't retaliate are often victims of further aggression and teased for being a punk.

In one of our nation's penitentiaries a male inmate, convicted of a violent offense, shared a personal story that underscores this dilemma. When he was young, the family moved frequently and he was always the "new kid on the block." This made him a ripe target. In fact, he said: "Sometimes I wondered if I was wearing a shirt that said 'Bullies apply' because every time I started a new school some boys would start punching me." He was particularly vulnerable when he stepped off the bus so he acquired one skill very quickly—sprinting. One day, he ran breathlessly into his house and found his father at home. When his father asked why he was so short of breath, he explained the reason. With that, his father took him into the front yard and beat him much harder than any kids had ever done. His father threatened to give the boy the same punishment if he ever ran away from a fight again. The boy had believed that running away was preferable to fighting. The lesson he learned from his father was that he was supposed to fight, and if he didn't, he was a coward. Today, he is in a state prison, serving a twelve-year sentence for assault.

This message is one that fathers often give to their sons and needs to be explored as we look for solutions to the problem of bullying. Acquiring a social norm that values walking away from a fight will require a major shift in social attitudes about character and strength.

Jay Winsten has embarked on an ambitious campaign to do just that. It was Winsten who came up with the concept of the Designated Driver that has clearly changed the drinking and driving habits of millions of Americans. Fresh from that extraordinary success, he is now trying to address the issue of teenage homicide. Winsten theorizes that even small disagreements can lead to shootings if nothing occurs to defuse the anger. He was looking for a strategy that could interrupt an escalating situation and found it by listening to teen gang members discuss their feelings about the rampant violence in their lives. As a result he heard the phrase: "Squash it!" and is now working to persuade other teenagers to own the concept and accompany the cooling-off expression with a catchy hand sign. To make the sign, you form your left hand into a fist with the thumb facing up and use your flat right hand to put a lid, so to speak, on top of your fist. A campaign is being designed to capture the interest of young people and offer them an alternative.

The violence permeating the experience of today's teenagers can perhaps best be understood by considering the variety of contexts in which it occurs. Returning to our model of concentric circles of influence, specific individual traits and environmental characteristics may make some teenagers more likely to be violent. Adolescence is a period of biological and psychological transformation; hormonal changes produce dramatic physical growth, new and confusing sexual urges, and emotional swings that are difficult to manage. As challenging as the normal developmental changes are for the typical adolescent, some teenagers may be more biochemically vulnerable because of their genetic makeup and thus even more likely to act out their anger.

Don was a fraternal twin in a family of three other children. His parents described him as a fussy baby who had been harder to soothe and calm than any of their other children. He was irritable and impulsive. Don's parents found him challenging to raise, and the early years included some tough, but manageable terrain for the family. At adolescence, however, Don's anger came to a head and he was frequently embroiled in conflicts with teachers, peers, and family members. He was clearly a bully. It was not possible to attribute his difficulties to any one single source, but it appeared that Don had a "shorter fuse," a greater propensity to experience anger and act on it than his siblings, including his fraternal twin. Although the relative influence of "nature" and "nurture" is difficult to distinguish, in Don's case it seems that his inborn temperament contributed significantly to his interpersonal problems. Counseling helped Don learn techniques to manage his anger. When Don first entered therapy he described his anger as functioning like a light switch: one moment it was off, and then the next moment it suddenly was on. In therapy Don learned that his anger actually developed gradually over time, but he did not become conscious of it until it was at full boil. Don learned to monitor his anger, frequently asking himself how angry he was on a scale of one to ten. He learned techniques to cool off, to walk away from the situation when his anger was at a much lower, more manageable level.

Crack babies, infants with Fetal Alcohol Syndrome, and some children with Attention Deficit Hyperactivity Disorder (ADHD) are other examples of children with disruptive behavior patterns that may have a biological basis. The irritability, impulsivity, and learning deficiencies associated with each of these syndromes can interfere with peer relationships.

Family variables can play a powerful role in the aggression. A case in point is the story of a five-year-old boy, Mike, who is the terror of his day-care center. He is constantly lashing out at other children and when he plays with toys, he smashes them together in a violent way. Sister Berta, who administers the center, has also become his foster mother. She has chosen to keep him in her home because she knows the background of this extremely aggressive child. He was witness to the brutal murder of his three-year-old-sister—stomped to death by their father. When Mike misbehaves, Sister Berta does not spank him. She does not intend to perpetuate the violence he experienced. She will wrap him in a blanket, or hold him for as long as he will allow, but she despairs of his ever responding to nonpunitive discipline. There are scars on his back that have yet to heal from belt buckle beatings inflicted long ago. Even her unconditional love is not enough to reverse the consequences of his father's cruelty—at least, not yet.

Lenore Walker, author of *The Battered Woman*, reports that children who are not physically abused themselves but witness violence suffer a more insidious form of child abuse. Mike will have to deal with the scars of his psyche as well as his body.

School environment is also an important factor. The incidence of violence is increasing as the size of school classes increase. Crowding, anonymity, and a greater sense of alienation are variables that some researchers believe are related to aggression. Gordon and Isiah were shot and killed at point-blank range by another student in a hall at a New York high school in the early '90s. They were two of the seventy students who were killed, shot, stabbed, or permanently injured on the school grounds in the last four years. One student was quoted as saying: "Around here, kids carry guns like other people carry cigarettes."

A tragic example of the influence of community is the death in February, 1994, of Michael Davis, a journalism student and junior at a southern Missouri State University. At least eleven young men are under criminal investigation for the hazing incident that led to Davis's death. In the last twenty years, there have been more than fifty-one deaths from fraternity hazing and pledge-related activities, says Hank Nuwer, hazing researcher.

Paul, a fraternity hazing victim, was kidnapped, taken to a bar, and forced to drink what he calls "ridiculous amounts of alcohol." As a guest on a national talk show, he tried to explain the humiliation and torture that is part of the hazing process. "Fraternities and brothers that have been involved with a fraternity for several years, or even several semesters feel that by torturing you, by disciplining you, it makes you stronger as a group. And when you're pledging, you lose your individuality, or you're supposed to lose your individuality and become a member of your group, which is your pledge class."

Jared, another hazing victim, described the peer pressure: ". . . even though you're not forced and bound and gagged to do something, it's like your duty. You do what the other members in the fraternity want you to do. They did it. If you didn't do it, then you wouldn't really be a full member, then would you? I mean, if everybody else had gone through something and I was to say, 'No, I don't want to do this,' then I wouldn't feel like I earned it. I wouldn't feel like I earned my status as an active."

Anthropologists have observed that almost all cultures have physically demanding rites and rituals to mark the passage from childhood to adulthood. Our Western culture is a notable exception. In *The Power of Myth*, a series of conversations between mythologist Joseph Campbell and journalist Bill Moyers, Moyers said "[Modern] society has provided adolescents with no rituals by which they become members of the tribe, of the community. All children need to be twice born, to learn to function rationally in the present world, leaving childhood behind." Perhaps the pledging process for new fraternity members and initiation requirements for gangs, despite their obvious differences, are concrete, specific examples of adolescents' attempts to initiate each other into a new developmental stage. In this light, bullying could be seen as a less formal and less highly ritualized attempt by adolescents to create their own rites of passage. Perhaps this might explain our puzzling reluctance to take the problem of bullying seriously. On some level, perhaps, we intuitively recognize bullying as a way of "toughening up" children, preparing them to take on the many responsibilities and challenges of adulthood. Mary Pipher, Ph.D., addresses one aspect of this phenomenon in the book *Reviving Ophelia: Saving the Selves of Adolescent Girls*. She describes the pressure adolescent girls place on each other to dress in a particular way, to adopt particular conversational styles, and to make particular choices about friends and activities as part of the "rigorous training for the female role." These pressures to conform are often enforced by isolating the young woman who insists on carving out her own role.

If in fact our children and teenagers are telling us they need some way to mark the passage from childhood to adulthood we must also be able to hear that their rituals are not working. The fragile state of many families, the easy accessibility of handguns, and the glossy, idealized images of violence without consequences that pervade the culture have changed the situation dramatically. We are challenged as a community to create meaningful, healthy rites of passage that mark this important developmental process.

Perhaps the personal observations of Paul and Jared, two victims who were cowed by the group ethic, can give us some insight into the tremendous power that takes over when the "community" comes into play. Their stories also point up the normal desire for rituals and tribal initiation rites that mark the childhood rites of passage.

One of the most frightening examples of community malignancy is the phenomena of violent youth gangs. Whether it be a fraternity or a gang, there is inordinate pressure put on members of the group to conform to the code. In Wichita, Kansas, law enforcement officials reported that initiation rites for several gangs included three requirements—to assault a police officer, to rob a home while someone was in the house, and to rape a woman. When drugs and guns are added to the equation, drive-by shootings become a common occurrence instead of an unthinkable act.

The cultural impact on behavior is tied to the glorification of violence in the media. Speaking from his prison cell in North Carolina, a nineteen-year-old juvenile offender recalled in a *Time* magazine article that when he and his friends became bored with television and each other, they would look for someone to beat up. "We hit them, kicked them, just beat them up. It was something teenagers do. You just be excited. You might see a gang on TV beating up on somebody . . . if a person looked at us funny, we'd go pick on that person."

The average child watches up to 8,000 made-for-television murders and 100,000 acts of violence by the end of grade school. A *USA Today*/CNN/Gallop Poll on the entertainment industry, published in *USA Today* on June 8, 1995, showed the following results: 83 percent of respondents think the entertainment industry should make a serious effort to reduce sex and violence in movies and music and on television. Sixty-three percent of respondents believe that reducing the amount of sex and violence in movies and music and on television would significantly improve the moral climate of the USA.

The debate on media violence will continue to rage. Censorship, freedom of speech, First Amendment rights will be rallying cries. Boys will be boys, cartoons will be cartoons, and violence will be subsidized by sponsors and consumers.

In summary, our greatest problem is our indifference to the consequences of physical cruelty. It is the repetition of denial that has allowed us to turn our backs on abused children, battered partners, exploited elderly, and bullied youths. Adults tend to underestimate the effects of bullying behavior.

To gain insight, we must acknowledge that some individuals have a greater predisposition to aggressive behavior because of genetic or prenatal factors. Similarly, the family environment plays a profound role in the development of appropriate versus aggressive behavior.

Schools become the arena where these influences collide, creating a climate of terror for too many young people. Metal detectors alone will not resolve the complicated interactions that surface daily. Just as schools have been targeted for serious education about the effects of drug abuse, a plan must be put in place that assures students a safe environment.

One of the major life-skill tasks for adolescent boys is establishing a strong sense of masculinity. An increasing number of boys who are growing up in homes without fathers are using Rambo-like characters as their models for masculine behavior. Movie heroes and musical entertainers become substitute role models for absent fathers, which causes many young men to confuse aggression with masculinity—to their own detriment as well as ours.

The proliferation of guns and entertainment violence must be included as a factor in any perspective of the bullying issue. The cultural influences on bullies' actions cannot be isolated anymore than the family relationships, the school code, the community atmosphere, and genetic factors. Here are some ideas for consideration:

- We must relinquish the myth that physical bullying is not a concern and make it clear to children that such behavior is unacceptable.
- Children's reports of physical bullying must be taken seriously.
- Fathers or other male role models need to talk to their sons about alternatives to fighting. Young men need to know they can obtain approval without resorting to violence.
- Firearms in the hands of children who lack the responsibility to handle dangerous weapons should be banned.
- Policies that prohibit hazing should be enforced on all college campuses.
- Media violence must be challenged and parents should exert authority over the quantity and quality of exposure to violent programming by their children.

CHAPTER FOUR

Verbal Abuse

"Sticks and stones can break your bones . . ."

VERBAL ABUSE IS the most common form of bullying. In this chapter we will attempt to define verbal abuse, share some anecdotal material, and present the reasons why we believe that sticks and stones can break your bones, but words can break your heart.

When we do training sessions with students, we always begin the session by asking them to complete the following statement: "Sticks and stones can break your bones, but . . ." Invariably, the group response is: ". . . names can never hurt you." We wonder how many generations of children have memorized this saying—counting on it to be true, only to be betrayed by the myth.

In 1977, I was invited to be part of a panel discussion on child abuse. Marilyn, a member of Parents Anonymous, shared the speaker's platform with me and was very open about her experiences in the self-help group for abusive parents. She spoke of her "target" child, the daughter who most reminded her of herself; how long it had taken for her to recognize her own abusive behavior; and the support she received from the other members.

During the question-and-answer period, she was asked if she would disclose how she had abused her child. In the late '70s, the topic of child abuse was still mysterious and verboten. *The Battered Child* by Dr. C. Henry Kempe and Dr. Ray Helfer, published in 1968 had catapulted the subject from professional discourse to social intercourse but there were only a few courageous people who were willing to publicly disclose the fact that they had abused their children.

I had heard Marilyn speak on numerous occasions and no one had ever dared to ask her the question that was on all of our minds. "I am a verbal abuser," she replied. There was a collective gasp in the audience. Verbal abuse was never considered in any of the definitions of child abuse that had become the center of public discussion. In 1977, the physical abuse and neglect of children was a shock to our senses and caused disbelief. We struggled to understand and accept the dynamics that would move a parent to batter his or her own child. I had imagined Marilyn wielding a belt or a stick on her daughter. Surely brutality was a criteria for joining a group like Parents Anonymous, I thought.

Marilyn described the circumstances that led to the recognition of herself as an abusive parent. She worked as a counselor at a juvenile detention center. One day a mother of one of the juvenile offenders visited her son and immediately launched into a verbal tirade that could be heard by everyone on the floor. Marilyn watched the young man shrink in humiliation as his peers witnessed the tongue-lashing. She felt tears welling in her eyes. At first she cried for the son and then she cried for her own daughter, recalling all the times she had embarrassed her in similar fashion.

While a member of P.A., Marilyn observed that parents who physically abused their children did so sporadically while parents who verbally abused their children did so chronically. Then she went on to say that "the scars of the soul take a lot longer to heal than the scars of the flesh." To this day, I have not heard a more profound statement about word power.

THE VARIOUS KINDS OF VERBAL ABUSE

We are defining verbal abuse as the use of words as cruelty to a child's physical, moral, or mental well-being. To illustrate various types of verbal abuse we will draw from the themes that emerged from our survey:

1. Verbal abuse intends to harm, to cause pain.
2. Verbal abuse involves intensity and duration.
3. Verbal abuse is used to gain power over another person.
4. Verbal abuse attacks the vulnerability of the victim.
5. Verbal abuse leaves a victim feeling isolated and exposed.
6. Verbal abuse escalates, leading to physical consequences.
7. Verbal abuse is a form of sexual harassment.

Let's look at each of these forms of verbal abuse with a specific example.

Verbal Abuse Intends to Harm, to Cause Pain

As we look at the impact of verbal abuse on young people the hurtful aspect is undeniable. The following are excerpts from a column by Jennifer Howe, published in the Kansas City Star.

> One morning last week, ten-year-old Christian Rodriguez woke up full of dread. He just couldn't go back to school.
>
> "Lots of kids teased me every hour of the day," he said. "They really got me to a point where I couldn't hold it in anymore."
>
> So he emptied his piggy bank and sneaked bread, potato chips, and soda out of the kitchen.
>
> "I was thinking about my parents and my dog," said Christian. It might be a long time before he saw them again, he thought. He slipped a photo of his parents into his book bag.
>
> When his parents went to check on him at 7 A.M., he was gone.
>
> Christian hunkered down in the back seat of an abandoned station wagon a few blocks from home. Police searched house-to-house and into the night.

"I thought I was going to die," said his mother, Ana Rodriguez. The next morning a woman recognized Christian from media reports as he walked past her house. She took him home.

"I love you and Daddy," he told his mother, "but I knew you would make me go to school."

Christian is not sure why the kids at school began picking on him. His mother thinks it's because he gets good grades.

"They just said a lot things," Christian said. "I used to cry about it. I'd ask them if they would stop teasing me. I'd ask real nicely, but then it would get worse."

It is quite common for bullying victims to blame themselves for the labels they acquire from their peers, even when those qualities stem from genetic or physiological sources that are beyond the victim's control. When she was a ninth grader, Angie Erickson wrote an essay that was published in *Newsweek* magazine, October 24, 1994. Angie is a twin. Her sister has no birth defects but Angie was born with cerebral palsy. When they were young, Angie's disabilities were not as noticeable, but when she reached school age and couldn't write or speak like everyone else, other students said she talked really weird and called her "a retard."

Every time someone was mean to me, I would start to cry and I would always blame myself for being different.

When I was twelve, my family moved. I kept this fairy tale in my head that, at my next school, no one would be mean to me or would see that I had a disability. I'd always wished I could be someone other than myself. I found out the hard way that I wasn't going to change, that I'd never be able to write and run with no problems. When kids in my new school found that I couldn't write and my talking and walking were out of the ordinary, they started making fun of me. They never took time to know me. Everything went back to the way it was before. I went back to blaming myself and thinking that, since I was different, I'd never fit in. I would cry all the time, because it was so hard for me to make friends again. I didn't know whether I should trust anyone—I thought that if people know that I had a disability they would not like me anymore.

Verbal Abuse
Involves Intensity and Duration

William is a fourteen-year-old boy in a suburban school district whose offense is taking dancing lessons. William enjoys dancing as well as other cultural activities. He is not particularly interested in sports and his artistic nature apparently exasperates his peers. They began expressing their irritation with him by calling him "fag" and "homo." He tried ignoring their taunts but they continued calling him the same names with a few variations thrown in. When they tired of name calling, they began making up riddles that linked crude questions with obscene answers. They made up poems that rhymed with the word "faggot" and never missed any opportunity to embarrass him. Every day he could count on the jeering language that mocked him. In my last conversation with William's mother, she was trying desperately to get school authorities to intervene. William, like several other young men we have spoken with, will probably give up studying dance. The peer pressure is too intense.

Verbal Abuse Is
Used to Gain Power over Another Person

Gina and Trish were academic competitors since elementary school. They both made straight A's. Whenever there was a test, Trish always wanted to know how Gina did, hoping for an opportunity to gloat. Trish did everything she could to destroy Gina's self-esteem. When she couldn't win an argument, she would resort to other means to demean Gina. There was the day she announced that her mother didn't think she should spend time with her anymore. For no apparent reason, she would approach Gina in the halls and start yelling at her in front of other friends. Gina's embarrassment cannot be minimized nor can the fear that, on any given day, the degrading event might reoccur. Trish could not tolerate a rival and when she could not compete and win fairly, she was quite willing to use devious, verbally abusive ways to hold power over her classmate.

Verbal Abuse Attacks
the Vulnerability of the Victim

Barry got off on the wrong tack when he was in middle school. When his parents divorced, his mother remarried, and his step-father's solution to every discipline issue was to beat Barry. Barry's response was to get in fights at school and become part of the drug scene. For several years he maintained his reputation as a troublemaker until he finally dropped out of school. He was fortunate that a girlfriend, her family, and church youth group came into his life. Barry underwent a remarkable conversion in his attitudes about himself and others. Even though he was now two years older than other students in his class, he reentered school with new convictions and clear goals. His experiences had taught him a great deal about how to negotiate adolescent land mines but he was not completely immune to the manipulation of his peers. His explosive temper had sabotaged him many times. As determined as he was not to fight, there were students who were equally determined to reduce him to his earlier trigger-quick responses. They were dogged in trying to discover his "Achilles heel." But no matter what names they called him, no matter how hard they tried to provoke him, they could not penetrate his resistance. He deflected every personal attack. Ultimately, however, they found his only hot button. They called his mother a whore, and Barry lost control. In spite of all his attempts at will power, Barry succumbed when they insulted his mother. When Barry discerned their sense of triumph, he finally put the last piece of his struggle in place and chose never to give them the power to goad him again.

Verbal Abuse Leaves a
Victim Feeling Isolated and Exposed

Most childhood taunting and teasing is overt. However, some bullies are quite capable of engaging in brainwashing techniques.

Whenever Rae would spend time with Shandra, she would come away feeling sad or depressed. She considered Shandra to be one of her closest friends, and they were involved in a church group together. In fact, it was Shandra who invited Rae to become a member, but then she "confided" to her that no one had wanted her to join. When Rae got her driver's license, she was the first one in the church group who was able to drive. Again, Shandra confided to her that people were being nice to her, just so they could get rides. Shandra not only used subtle techniques to undermine Rae's confidence in herself, she did it in a very "sincere and caring" way. The result was that Rae became very distrustful and confused about her ability to have genuine relationships. Rae pulled away from the church group and became a loner, like so many other students who have been damaged by the words of others.

Verbal Abuse Escalates, Leading
to Physical Consequences

A recent, horrendous example began at a Friday night football game between two suburban high schools. According to a newspaper report, the victors decided to rub salt in the wounds of the losing team by taunting their opponents. The exchange of insults grew into a full-blown fight and a challenge to continue the contest over the weekend. Plans were made to meet at a park on Sunday but when their rivals did not appear, the disappointed students drove to their opponents' high school where a pickup football game was in play. While forty or fifty students brawled, a car drove up and a student, who observed that his classmates were outnumbered and overwhelmed, fired a gun. Two teens died, four others were wounded and a seventeen-year-old suspect will be tried for murder. A typical team rivalry led to taunting words and ended with fatal wounds. Students from the two schools are meeting to do some healing work and make sure that such an incident will never occur again.

Verbal Abuse Is a
Form of Sexual Harassment

Gossip is frequently mentioned by young people as a form of bullying that is dominated by females. Rumors, stories, "he said, she said" tales seem to be the abuse of choice for many girls but our example was instigated by a rejected suitor.

Rachel had no idea that Jonah had scratched the words "Rachel is a slut" in the boys' bathroom. If it weren't for her cousin, she might never have discovered why her boyfriend suddenly ignored her and boys made snide, sexual remarks when she walked down the hallway. Her reputation as an easy mark was established with a penknife in a restroom stall and the fact that it was not true could not stop the tide of gossip that swept her school. Overnight her happy, secure world was upended. Her boyfriend and even some of the girls in her social network avoided her, without giving her any clue or opportunity to defend herself against the malicious graffiti. With the support of two friends, Rachel survived the devastating experience, but she will never forget the disillusionment and depression that consumed her senior year.

STUDENT FOCUS GROUPS ON VERBAL ABUSE

When I first began talking to elementary school students about verbal abuse, I told them of a memo that had come across my desk stating that the average child received 213 put-downs a week. I asked for feedback—was their experience more, less, or about the same. Invariably, they would divide 213 put-downs by seven and come up with thirty a day. They would add the names they were called on the bus, at recess, in the cafeteria, in gym class, after school, by siblings and came to the conclusion that thirty was about average. I then asked them to tell me the kind of names they were called so we could list them on the blackboard. Some of the names were the same ones that were popular fifty years ago, such as "four eyes," "metal mouth," "retard." There were also new ones—"dork," "geek," "nerd," and a few children privately told me about a category of vulgar and obscene words that I will leave to your imagination. What shocked me, even more than the words themselves, was the age at which the members of my group first heard them (first grade) and the age at which they understood the meaning (second grade).

They went on to explain that dirty words had little effect—they were just fun to repeat. The personal, derogatory names had much more impact and the names that hurt the most were the ones directed at family members. One young girl who lived in a fairly affluent community was most vulnerable when her classmates would tease her because her mother worked as a waitress.

One morning, I spoke to a session of first, second, and third graders. I went through my usual routine about sticks and stones, some of the tragic stories that had begun with words, and involved the class in making the traditional blackboard list. I worked hard to impress them with the consequences of teasing and the role they could play in eliminating this problem. At the end of the session, I asked how many of them would make a pledge not to call anyone a name again. All hands were raised and I was quite excited about my success. Then I met with the fourth, fifth, and sixth graders. We went over the same material and reached the magic moment when I asked for the pledge. Out of more than one hundred students, three hands went up. Recovering from my deflation, I thanked them for being honest with me and acknowledged that it certainly would have been easier to give the "guest speaker" the answer she wanted. I then asked the students to tell me why they could not make such a pledge in face of the discussion we had had about the pain that words can cause. They were quite open about admitting that they could not possibly imagine going through a day without name calling.

When I ask students to recommend strategies to combat verbal abuse they suggested ignoring, retaliating, letting the perpetrator know that you are hurting, discussing it with a friend, making a joke about it, and reporting the situation to an adult. Few students believed that letting the perpetrator know that you are hurting will stop the abuse. In fact, many felt it would only further incite the bully to "get to you." Younger students are more inclined to report the situation to an adult. Older students believe that reporting puts the victim at greater risk for revenge, but should be considered as a last resort.

One boy who has prominent buck teeth handles the situation by preempting the verbal attack. He refers to himself as a "chipmunk" and makes accompanying noises. Before anyone can label him, he uses humor to protect himself.

A conversation with students from a wealthy, suburban public high school was very disturbing. The school parking lot was filled with expensive cars—NOT the property of the teachers. In the past year one student committed suicide, several students were hospitalized for drug overdosing, fights were commonplace, police and drug sniffing dogs were part of the school scene.

The students that I spoke with estimated that over 50 percent, possibly 75 percent of the kids were using some kind of drug, mostly marijuana, "to get away from the pressure and stress of daily school life."

"What kind of pressures are driving students from upper middle class families to take drugs?" I asked.

"They can't handle the verbal abuse," was the response. "Kids are hateful." "Girls are called fat slobs, bitches, sluts, and whores. I know one girl who is overweight who spends most of the day in tears." "You don't ever get used to the insults." "It's scary to be around people who are so mean." "If you have a boyfriend, you're a slut, if you don't have a boyfriend, you're a lesbian." "One day, a boy unzipped my backpack in class, grabbed my sanitary napkins and started tossing them around the room."

Some of the male students are disgusted with the behavior of their peers and try to stand up for females and males who are being victimized, but they admit it's a lost cause.

When I asked about adult intervention they were very outspoken about the failure of teachers and administrators to intervene. "Teachers tell you to come to them to talk about your problems, but when you do, they don't really want to hear what you have to say. They don't have time to deal with all the kids who are messed up on drug and alcohol."

As for parents, one student said she thought that parents would be astonished and outraged if they knew what the reality of school life was like. She also reported that students who might be inclined to disclose the drug scene to their parents had received death threats and she was not willing to dismiss the possibility.

We have spoken with a number of teenagers who question a campaign against verbal abuse. They accuse us of taking the fun out of childhood and living a boring life. Once I was asked how I felt about teasing that is good-natured and causes no pain. I turned the question back to the class and was pleased with the thoughtful responses. Several students focused on the alleged painlessness. The discussion went like this:

First Student: "How do you know the person being teased isn't suffering?"

Second student: "Because they don't get mad or ask me to stop."

Third student: "What if they are just pretending not to care in hopes that you'll leave them alone?"

Fourth student: "What if they didn't believe you would stop if they asked you to?"

More of these discussions need to take place and students should be encouraged to express their concerns and strategies about this all too familiar problem in a safe atmosphere. Younger students are more willing to acknowledge that name calling is almost an addiction among peers and can cause as much or more pain than physical abuse.

Name calling is not restricted to children. Many political campaigns, conducted by mature adults, set a poor example for the younger generation. One way to make our turbulent world more gentle would be to calm our language. An exercise we recommend to raise awareness about the preponderance of violent metaphors in our conversation is to monitor your language for expressions such as: "The thought struck me" or "That play was a knockout" or "I'll take a shot at that question." Listen to your casual phrases with an ear for violent words. Every time we substitute a non-violent word and gentlize conversation, we become more conscious of the discipline required to modify language, and if we can change our language, then perhaps we can change our behavior.

In summary, there are different forms of verbal abuse. It can be obvious or very subtle. It can be disguised as sincere concern. It can be "in your face" hurtful or it can be behind your back gossip. It can be constant or it can be unpredictable. It can be hostility disguised as jokes. It can be untruthful accusations. The power of words to denigrate cannot be underestimated. And more often than not, verbal abuse escalates and can lead to physical abuse.

Some recommendations for dealing with verbal abuse:

- Adults need to impress young people that name-calling, teasing, and gossip can be damaging.
- Adults need to advise children that verbal abuse can escalate into more violent forms.
- Adults need to warn youngsters that verbal abuse can be camouflaged to appear as concern.

- Victims need to know that they do not deserve to be teased.
- Students with disabilities or differences of any kind are ripe targets for verbal abuse and deserve special protection by adults.
- Young people need to have a repertoire of strategies to deal with verbal abuse, including reporting or ignoring the abuse, asserting or confronting it, and using humor to deflect it.

CHAPTER FIVE

Emotional Abuse

"All children are cruel."

THIS CHAPTER WILL clarify emotional abuse as defined by James Garbarino, Ph.D., Edna Guttmann, and Janis Seeley, co-authors of *The Psychologically Battered Child*. Emotional abuse includes rejecting, terrorizing, ignoring, isolating, and corrupting. It is the most difficult form of bullying for children to understand.

"We must renounce the lie that emotional abuse prepares children for a hard life in a tough world. I've met some people who were prepared for a hard life that way—I met them while they were DOING life," states Andrew Vachss, author of "Down In the Zero," and "You Carry The Cure In Your Own Heart" in the August 28, 1994, issue of *Parade* magazine. Certainly, not all children who are emotionally abused will end up in prison, but Vachss statement causes us to examine the consequences of this insidious form of bullying with the same seriousness that we assign to physical and sexual abuse.

Vachss goes on to say "Emotional abuse is the systematic diminishment of another. It may be intentional or subconscious (or both), but it is always a course of conduct, not a single event. It is designed to reduce a child's self-concept to the point where the victim considers himself unworthy—unworthy of respect, unworthy of friendship, unworthy of the natural birthright of all children—love and protection."

A definition of emotional abuse must include the active as well as the passive components, often referred to as the sins of commission as well as the sins of omission. The withholding of relationship can be far more punitive than any act of meanness. The nature of this form of abuse makes it more elusive to determine. As state laws dealing with child abuse were passed, professionals were mandated to report suspected cases of child physical abuse and neglect. Many added sexual abuse, but few states included emotional abuse in their original statutes. It is extremely difficult for protective service investigators to confirm such accusations and even more challenging to prove in courtrooms.

As one child advocate, Dorothy Dean stated, "Emotional abuse is the most difficult type of abuse to define and diagnose. Physical abuse, and some sexual abuse, involves tangible or observable evidence which can be documented and verified. The victim, if old enough, can describe what occurred. Emotional abuse, however, is intangible. The wounds are internal but they may be more devastating and crippling than any other form of abuse."

Garbarino's five forms of psychological maltreatment—rejecting, terrorizing, ignoring, isolating, and corrupting is based on parents' interactions with their children, but there is a great deal of information from his studies that can be adapted to our focus on youth peer interactions.

Garbarino highlights different forms of psychological or emotional abuse in each of the major stages in the first eighteen years of life: infancy (birth to age two), early childhood (ages two to five), school age (five to eleven), and adolescence (eleven to eighteen). We will focus on emotional abuse in school age and adolescent children. In addition to being developmentally specific, Garbarino further characterizes all incidents as "mild," "moderate," and "severe." He describes "mild" abuse as those behaviors that cause psychological damage confined to one aspect of functioning such as a lack of confidence in public settings (such as the girl who gave up singing), "moderate" abuse such as those instances of maltreatment that may prevent a child from achieving success in important settings, such as school (the case of a boy who stopped trying to make good grades), and "severe" abuse such as those instances of maltreatment that will, in all likelihood, cause children to be crippled in one or more of life's primary settings—work, love, and play.

REJECTING

Where would you put the situation of the woman who cringes every February 14? While the world is decking itself out in red-and-white ribbons, while floral shops and candy stores are doing landoffice business, Nedra wants to curl up in bed and sleep the day away. Nedra was a stutterer. Every sentence was a challenge. No one wanted to wait to hear her struggle with her words. In third grade, in Miss Borgen's class, Valentines' Day was a "big deal." The students spent almost two weeks decorating their empty shoe boxes, looking forward to the special day when everyone in the class would slip their love messages into the waiting slits of their classmates' colorful containers. Nedra remembers that she insisted that her mother buy a valentine for everyone in the class and she carefully signed her name to each card. When the moment of celebration arrived, everyone scurried around the classroom, delivering their valentines with giggles of pleasure and embarrassment. Nedra was so busy making sure each person received her valentine, she didn't realize that she did not receive a single valentine until she returned to her seat and lifted the lid of her beautiful box. The memory never faded. Was that experience mild or moderate?

A clear example of severe rejection is an excerpt from an article by Jean Haley, reprinted with permission from the *Kansas City Star*, March 4, 1987.

> I remember the fat girl in my elementary school. With shame.
> The little building was filled with a fairly average collection of

bright, aggressive, noisy, imitative country kids, and we made her days miserable from the time she was dropped off in her father's big car to the end of the stuffy afternoon.

We never bothered to really find out much about her. Her size, which was grossly large, was too obvious. Even without that barrier, her appearance was different. It was said her family originated in Eastern Europe, cause enough in our minds to both explain her stubborn size and earn her even more derision.

She got far more attention than the most popular boy or girl in school. She was called the usual names mercilessly tossed at heavy children. The boys poked and pulled her hair or dress sashes, then ran and laughed at a safe distance. The girls systematically excluded her from "clubs" and the "secret language" we periodically dreamed up.

There were snickers when she walked by and sneers when she was asked to demonstrate an arithmetic lesson or read from the reading book. We whispered about what was probably in her lunch and eyed her when she marched to teacher's desk. We smirked when she made a mess of a lesson, which she did repeatedly.

How can a child defend herself against a campaign of whispers, giggles, and sneers? If someone were to strike her, or throw her to the ground she might feel justified in reporting such an attack. She might even have witnesses to confirm her claim. But how does she describe "snickering" in a compelling way? Or, more likely, will she just choose to suffer in silence?

ISOLATING

Isolating, according to Garbarino, is depriving children of normal occasions and opportunities for social interaction.

Sarah's case is an example of severe peer isolation. In third grade she moved to a new school and began to establish herself with her classmates. During the next two years she invaded the territory of elementary school power of two girls who had been unchallenged from the time they entered kindergarten. Teachers favored Sarah, giving her prominent parts in school plays. She excelled in her schoolwork, and most threatening of all, she was attracting attention from the popular boys. By fifth grade the two girls decided to teach Sarah a lesson and devised a sinister plan. They organized their classmates to isolate her from all interaction. No one was to speak to her, choose her to be on a team, call on her to read, or walk in the halls with her. She was to be ostracized from all contact. The mass psychology was very seductive and everyone supported the conspiracy—except for one girl, Cindy. At the age of eleven, Cindy was well on her way to becoming a musician and had developed the ability to think for herself and stand apart from the crowd.

Cindy was not very athletic and consequently team captains did not fight over her. She and Sarah would huddle together for the "picking" session and were consistently passed over, finally requiring the gym teacher to assign them to a team. Reading period was another crisis. Every afternoon, the teacher would call on a student to begin the oral reading. If it was a boy, when he finished his page, he was to call on a girl who then selected a boy to continue. Each day, the tortuous process would conclude with the teacher asking: "Is there anyone who hasn't been called on?" At first, Sarah would raise her hand and acknowledge that she hadn't had a turn, but as the weeks went by, she pretended that she hadn't heard the question. Cindy couldn't rescue Sarah from the alternate gender reading ritual and there was always someone in the class who was gleeful to point out that Sarah hadn't been chosen.

Every recess, every gym class, every reading session was a painful, humiliating reminder of her excommunication from her former friends. Cindy remained loyal, in spite of her parent's counsel that Sarah wouldn't be her best friend anymore if the "in crowd" changed their mind and welcomed her back. Sarah's mother was sympathetic but unsure of what she could do to intervene in the follies of fifth-grade perils so she counted on Cindy to be her daughter's buffer against the isolation. It is hard to imagine that the teacher never caught on to the mass abandonment of Sarah. But she never interfered.

At the beginning of sixth grade, the bullies decided that Sarah had been punished enough. Her year-long embargo was lifted and she was allowed to resume her role with the popular crowd. Cindy's parents were right. Sarah no longer had time for Cindy.

A similar example with a different reason and a different outcome was told to us by Annette. It all began when Annette heard that there was going to be a birthday celebration for her friend, Sheila. She was unaware that it was a surprise party and she approached Sheila to let her know that she hadn't received an invitation. The girls who had sent out the invitations were so angry at Annette for spoiling the surprise that they decided to ostracize her. Because her life was made miserable by this intentional alienation, she did everything she could to return to their good graces. Her pleas were met with on-going silent rejection and resolution came only when her concerned parents moved so that she could enroll at another school. The consequences of such social alienation take a terrible toll on the fragile egos of ten-year-old girls. Being blackballed from slumber parties is the kind of abuse that is not obvious to anyone except the heartbroken rejectee and, possibly, her parents.

TERRORIZING

Garbarino describes terrorizing for adolescents as threatening to reveal intensely embarrassing characteristics or exposing the child to public humiliation.

The following incident was the focus of a "Donahue" program, November 16, 1993.

Brian Seamons was the backup quarterback for his high school football team. One day as he came out of the locker room shower, he was dragged by five of his teammates and taped to a towel rack horizontal to the floor. The trainer tape was wrapped around his feet, his chest, his hands, and around his genitals. Then they brought in a young woman from the school, whom he happened to have dated on one occasion, to witness his humiliation. Brian's parents were appalled and supported him unconditionally through the ordeal that followed. In a series of unilateral decisions by the school principal, the coach, the school board, and ultimately by the superintendent, the team's participation in the regional playoffs was canceled as well as the opportunity to compete for the state high school championship.

There was great resentment from other players, students, cheerleaders, and parents who felt that the suspension of the post-season game was too severe a penalty for the kind of incident that is "part of the game" as one student stated. Other comments from students were: "It happens in sports. It happens in every school." "This has been going on ever since we were sophomores . . . no one ever told us not to do it." One parent observed that this kind of occurrence is all a bunch of fun, the kind of thing that should never have gone public beyond the locker room.

Brian claims he was kicked off of the football squad by the coach because he didn't apologize to the team for betraying them. The bitterness of the student body, who blamed him for the cancellation, further victimized him. Though Brian sought therapy to deal with the multitude of problems that grew out of "locker room fun," his scars will not disappear easily.

This example of emotional abuse illustrates the role that school and community can play in underestimating the seriousness of the problem. At the same time, Brian's parents were clear that the perpetrators, the coach, the angry parents, et al., were not bad people. They felt strongly that everyone who was involved—students, faculty, and parents were good people who allowed a situation to get out of hand. Without clear social consensus that such behavior is intolerable, and in fact constitutes abuse, reactions can become distorted and consequences blurred. Inappropriate behavior will continue to be condoned and innocent students will become scapegoats.

CORRUPTING

Corrupting is defined as encouraging a child's unsuitable behavior in the area of sexuality, aggression, or substance abuse.

Pete went to a party one evening and didn't like the way he was treated. He felt rejected and threatened by the guys who were there so he left and joined a group of his own friends. He started describing the party he had been to and began exaggerating the details of his treatment at the affair. By the time he had embellished the facts, his friends were as angry as he was.

Without giving serious thought to the consequences, Pete's friends followed him to the party and a fight ensued. Before the night was over, at least five people had to be taken to the hospital and several cars were damaged. Pete's friends were lucky that no one was killed. In return for paying restitution for hospital bills and car damage, the charges were dropped. Pete had made up stories about his experience in order to arouse his friends' loyalty. Based on his exaggerated description of the events, they became enraged and were ultimately involved in violent aggression.

The most devastating example in recent memory of a child who resisted corruption is the case of a five-year-old Chicago boy who was thrown from a fourteenth-floor window by two boys, aged ten and eleven. The older boys became angry with the youngster because he wouldn't steal candy for them so they lured Eric and his half-brother, Derrick into a vacant apartment. They dangled the small boy from a window ledge by his wrists while his half-brother tried desperately to save him. As he was holding Eric's arm, one of the boys bit Derrick on his hand and he lost his grip. Within seconds Eric plunged to his death.

For adults who are not privy to specific information, but suspect that children in their care are experiencing problems, the symptoms of emotional abuse include unusual anxiety and unrealistic fears; irrational and persistent fears, dread, or hatred; sleep problems, nightmares; and/or behavioral extremes.

To summarize, emotional abuse is the most difficult form of bullying for children to understand. Because it lacks the tangible evidence of physical or verbal abuse, children have a difficult time articulating the suffering they experience when classmates ostracize or withhold friendship. The need for peer acceptance is disproportionate for young people, which can make them very susceptible to pressures of all kinds.

James Garbarino, Ph.D., describes five operational types of emotional abuse: rejecting, terrorizing, ignoring, isolating, and corrupting. Within these patterns the intensity can vary from mild, to moderate, to severe. We did not give an example of ignoring as it relates to bullying because there is no way to compare the consequence of being ignored by a peer with the impact on an infant who is ignored by a parent.

We offer the following suggestions for consideration when dealing with emotional abuse:

- Adults need to discuss the different types of emotional abuse and impress upon children the damage that these behaviors can cause.
- Teachers should be on the lookout for ostracization. Such patterns may be more observable on the playground than in the classroom but an alert teacher can look for clues when any kind of partnering or group selection process is taking place.
- Parents could be more sensitive to the painful exclusion that can occur around birthday and slumber parties and discuss these situations with their children.

- Corruption can occur in many forms and a child who can pinpoint the practice may be better equipped to resist the pressure.

CHAPTER SIX

Sexual Abuse

"Take a look at those watermelons!"

OF ALL THE peer abuse issues, sexual abuse is by far the most complicated, the most difficult to document, and the hardest to address. There are a number of factors that set it apart from the physical, verbal, and emotional problems—as hurtful as those issues may be. In this chapter, we will analyze sexual bullying and clarify the difference between flirting and sexual harassment.

Let us begin with a definition of sexual abuse. In their preliminary report (National Adolescent Perpetrator Network, 1988), the Task Force on Juvenile Sexual Offending states: "Sexual interactions involving children with peers or younger children are problematic if the relationship is coercive, exploitive or aggressive or threatens the physical or psychological well-being of either participant." The report further declares that "the exploitive nature of child sexual offending is measured in terms of size and age differential; power or authority differential; lack of equality and consent; and threats, violence or aggression."

Many researchers count peer assaults, such as date rape as sexual abuse, while others exclude it unless there is a significant age difference.

According to David Finkelhor, prominent researcher at the University of New Hampshire, a definition of child sexual abuse requires two elements:

1. Sexual activities involving a child.
2. An abusive condition.

Sexual activities are divided into two categories. The first, noncontact abuse usually includes exhibitionism, voyeurism, verbal sexual propositions, or harassment. It can also include sexual notes or pictures, sexual graffiti, making suggestive or sexual gestures, pulling someone's clothes off, and spreading sexual rumors. The second category, contact sexual abuse, is further divided into sexual activity involving penetration and non-penetration sexual activity.

Finkelhor says that abusive conditions exist when:

1. The other person has a large age or maturational advantage over the child.
2. The other person is in a position of authority or in a caretaking relationship with the child.
3. The activities are carried out against the child using either force or trickery.

We would define nonabusive conditions as:

1. Sexual activities that occur when there is mutuality.
2. Experimentation with sexual language and words in a nondemeaning way.
3. Situations when children have equal power and authority.
4. An absence of coercion or manipulation.

Mutuality is a basic principle in nonabusive relationships, according to Janet Surrey and Stephen Bergman with the Stone Center for Developmental Services and Studies at Wellesley College. When mutuality is absent, the victim of sexual harassment, male or female, suffers serious trauma to self-concept and self-esteem.

Non-Contact Sexual Abuse

Non-contact sexual abuse includes exhibitionism, voyeurism, verbal, sexual propositions or harassment.

Christina was in eighth grade, three years ago, when she was first exposed to the pain of sexual innuendo. She stayed home for two days because of an illness. When she returned to school she was mortified to learn that her best friend had started a rumor that Christina was absent from school because she was pregnant. People that she didn't even know were coming up to her to ask about her pregnancy. Even the school administrators believed the rumor and she was given in-school suspension for three days. Her reputation was mangled by a lie and the lie was reinforced by school authorities. A young girl's social life can be very precarious when lies about her sexual activity are believed.

Another story came to me in the form of a letter.

When I was fifteen years old I lived in a small community where when something happens that night, the next day everyone and their dog knows what happened. Well, one night, me and my friends went over to these guys house and everyone was watching television and eventually one by one the bedrooms were being filled. Well, I didn't want to do anything so I didn't but the guy I was with was kind of expecting something. Well, when he didn't get anything, he went around telling everyone that the reason he didn't was because I smelled too bad. When I found out I went up to him and started yelling at him but he just laughed. For the next few weeks everyone got a kick out of making fun of me. I just said "yep" you're right and laughed at them and eventually someone else was being made fun of. So I do believe that if you agree or ignore them they'll leave you alone.

For Georgia, it began in kindergarten. There were several boys who chased her home from school every day, wanting to kiss her. For them it was sport; for Georgia it was horror. She could not run fast enough to escape them and she was repulsed by their lips on her face. She was no match for any one of the boys, much less their combined strength. There was not the slightest hint of affection in this kissing assault. Had there been any concern for Georgia, they surely would have stopped when she screamed, cried, pleaded, and tried to push them away. It was simply a matter of power, assumed by three boys at a very early age at the expense of a powerless little girl. Chances are that those boys, if questioned today would not be able to recall their behavior, but Georgia's memory of it has never disappeared. Now a grown woman, completing her Ph.D., she looks back on that terrifying ordeal as a defining experience. It was painful to Georgia that people whom she hoped would have concern for her could be completely indifferent to her needs. Perhaps even more damaging, however, was the confusion created for Georgia by the pairing of a kiss, a gesture associated with pleasure and affection, and the aggressive refusal to acknowledge her distress. Throughout grade school the harassment continued. Her parents could never understand why she refused to attend her brother's baseball games, a family event. She could never explain that one of her aggressors was the pitcher on the team. As an adult, the experience still haunts her. She continues to have difficulty sorting out the intentions of others, especially men, and has had problems establishing satisfying long-term relationships with men.

CONTACT SEXUAL ABUSE—PENETRATION

One of the most horrendous examples of contact sexual abuse occurred in a case that brought national shame to a community in which several members of the high school football team raped a female student with a broom handle. The girl was a special-education student and ill equipped intellectually or physically to deal with the coercive nature of the attack.

In another rape case, a fifteen-year-old boy kidnapped two twelve-year-old girls at gunpoint while they were on a trip to get candy. The girls said the kidnapper and another fifteen-year-old boy, used a .22 caliber pistol to force them to go to one of the boys' houses. Once there, one of the girls was told that she would be shot if she didn't have sex with the boy. At his trial, the boy defended himself by claiming that the twelve-year-old girl was a consenting partner and had an opportunity to escape. A doctor's testimony that the girl had injuries consistent with rape and police testimony of finding the pistol at the scene of the crime, convinced the jury to recommend an adult sentence of three life terms for the teenager. This case illustrates that sexual abuse can include physical, emotional, and verbal abuse.

CONTACT SEXUAL ABUSE—NON-PENETRATION

Cassie and Laverne would take turns playing at each other's homes after school. Sometimes they would do their fifth-grade homework together, sometimes they would play games, most often they would giggle and chatter about the topics that ten year olds find fascinating. One day, Laverne's older brother, Denny, was at home while they were harbored in Laverne's bedroom. It wasn't long before Denny knocked and asked if he could come in. At first, the girls were very flattered that a seventh grader would be interested in them and they were very welcoming. The first time Denny touched Cassie's breast she believed it was an accident and thought he would be embarrassed if she mentioned it so she said nothing. The next time he touched her, she realized that it was intentional and she looked to Laverne to control her brother's actions. Instead, Laverne joined her brother in encouraging Cassie to engage in sexual play with her brother and the two of them persuaded Cassie to touch Denny's penis. Cassie was caught up in a myriad of feelings ranging from loyalty to her friend, curiosity about Denny's genitals, guilt about participating in something that made her uncomfortable, and anger at the people whom she had trusted. After the fondling incident, Cassie left abruptly. She never played with Laverne again; never told her mother what happened, even when the nightmares persisted for months. She carried her "dirty" secret for a long time. It was many years before Cassie realized that many things she had done to punish herself, unconsciously, were related to the incident in Laverne's bedroom.

There are distinct gender issues that separate sexual harassment from physical, verbal, and emotional abuse. Boys and girls can describe, almost interchangeably, their responses to being punched, teased, or isolated. But it is more difficult for males to give credence to the sense of violation that sexual taunts create. The 1993 landmark study of the American Association of University Women, "Hostile Hallways," surveyed 1,632 students between grades eight and eleven. Eighty-five percent of girls and 76 percent of boys reported being sexually harassed at some point in school. Twenty percent of these students reported being victimized by an adult but 80 percent identified the harasser as another student. The harassment included everything from being touched or grabbed in a sexual way to being the object of jokes or sexual comments. It included being the target of bathroom graffiti or sexual rumors. When students were asked about the impact of harassment, girls were much more effected. For instance, the study showed that male and female students who reported sexual harassment experienced divergent emotional responses: embarrassment (girls 64 percent—boys 36 percent), self-consciousness (girls 52 percent—boys 21 percent), less confidence (girls 43 percent-boys 14 percent), fear (girls 39 percent—boys 8 percent). Outcomes as a result of the harassment were also quite different. Not wanting to go to school (girls 32 percent—boys 13 percent), staying home from school or cutting a class (girls 24 percent—boys 13 percent), making a lower grade on a test (girls 23 percent—boys 9 percent). In one area, their reactions were similar, however. Eighty-six percent of the students indicated that they would be "very upset" if they were called gay or lesbian (girls 87 percent—boys 85 percent). No other type of harassment, including physical abuse, provoked such a strong response from boys.

One effort to be as specific as possible about the behaviors that debase young people is the Harassment and Violence Policy developed by the Minnesota School Boards Association. There are nine elements: General Statement of Policy; Religious, Racial and Sexual Harassment and Violence Defined; Reporting Procedures; Investigation; School District Action; Reprisal; Right to Alternative Complaint Procedures; Harassment or Violence as Abuse; and Dissemination of Policy and Training. We will include the complete policy as an Appendix at the end of the book. Each school district in the state can use this policy as a model to develop their own policy statement. For instance, the harassment policy developed by the South Washington County Schools in Cottage Grove, MN, spelled out the following actions as constituting harassment:

1. Student bra snapping, giving "snuggies," or "pantsing" (pulling down boys' or girls' pants or pulling up girls' skirts).
2. Students "rating" other students.
3. Students displaying or circulating centerfolds or sexually explicit materials.
4. Name calling: "slut," "whore," "fag," lesbian," "cow," or "dog."
5. Teasing students about their sexual activities or lack of sexual activity.
6. Students wearing sexually offensive T-shirts, hats, or pins.
7. Displays of affection between students (i.e., "making out" in the halls).
8. Suggestive comments about apparel.

Sue Sattel, Gender Equity Specialist; Minnesota Department of Children, Families and Learning, reports that in Minnesota, school districts are encouraged to use their sexual, racial, and religious harassment policy to intervene on bullying when it includes racial and/or sexual slurs because bullying, per se, is not illegal but sexual harassment is. The object is to intervene, to encourage intervention; and to "treat" the victim and the perpetrator with educational material and assistance so that this behavior doesn't continue.

One option, therefore, is to draw on sexual harassment policies as a model for bullying intervention. Another option is to develop policies on bullying that include sexual harassment.

"Unfortunately, peer sexual harassment has not only increased, it has intensified, leading to a rise in sexual molestation committed by juveniles," states Rob Freeman-Longo, Director of the Safer Society Press.

While sexual abuse of children by adults has been thoroughly researched, sexual abuse of children by juveniles has been largely ignored.

In a publication by Carolyn Cunningham and Kee MacFarlane, "When Children Abuse," information is shared about a number of studies of juvenile sex offenders. In one 1984 study of 401 child sex abuse cases, 56 percent of the male child victims and 28 percent of the female child victims reported being abused by a juvenile offender. One study suggests that 30 to 50 percent of all child molestations are perpetrated by juveniles and a substantial percentage of adult offenders may begin their molesting behavior as juveniles.

Juvenile sexual offenders range in age from five to nineteen with median age between fourteen and fifteen. Juvenile sex offenders are representative of all ethnic, racial, and socioeconomic classes. Sexual abuse can include physical, verbal, and emotional components. Ninety percent of the juvenile offenders were male, and more than 60 percent of the sexual offenses involved penetration. Over 90 percent of the juvenile offenders selected a victim known to them, most commonly a seven- or eight-year-old.

Several characteristics of family environment have been described in the research literature on juvenile sex offenders. These include unstable home environments, sexual pathology within a parent, and the child viewing sexual interactions between parents or parent surrogates.

For younger students several factors blur an accurate picture of the extent of the problem. Many situations never come to light because of the secretive sexual explorations children engage in without understanding the nature of their actions. Adult taboos keep them ignorant of information they need. Children are frightened and fearful of their perpetrators, protecting their identity because of the usually severe threats to maintain secrecy. Some children who are being abused don't recognize it as such because it is often difficult for children to separate the pleasurable sensations from the violation. The indignity they experience is often eclipsed by the attention they receive. Then too, it is much more difficult to discuss this topic openly in classroom or family settings because of the stigmatization of sexual abuse. Children are less likely to volunteer information about their behavior as either perpetrators or victims.

On a "Prime Time Live" program about kids and sex, May 10, 1995, Diane Sawyer interviewed several elementary school teachers, a group of students, and parents with startling results. Any assumptions that sexual material in the media is going over the heads of young children were quickly dispelled. One teacher told of intercepting a love note passed between second-graders. One note said: "Let's get married." The written response was "Let's go to a hotel," and then on the back, "I want sex with you." Another teacher spoke of drawings of Cinderella and her prince by first and second graders showing Cinderella's breasts and nipples. Another teacher reported about a first-grade girl who couldn't be put at a desk sitting next to boys because when they shared reading books she would fondle them. There were additional stories of oral sex, masturbation, and second-graders found trying anal sex. If this doesn't give us a sense of urgency about the need to address sexual harassment in schools, I don't know what can.

Cunningham and MacFarlane have attempted to answer the question "Who are the sexually abusive children and why do they do the things they do?" In their book, they state:

They are male and female; they are black and white and brown. They live in the inner city, the best suburbs, and every place in between. Their parents may be insensitive, immature, abusive, or absent—or they may look like Ozzie and Harriet, the Huxtables, or the people next door. Some of these children are withdrawn and uncommunicative, others are outgoing, charming, and eager to please. Many have been sexually abused themselves, but some have not. Most reveal some history of physical, sexual, or emotional abuse, while others have been exposed to neglect or inappropriate behavior by adults or older siblings. Some have been raised in sexually overstimulating environments, some in homes where rigid sexual boundaries, strong religiosity, or unspoken family prohibitions left little room for the expression of conflicted thoughts or feelings. Of all the potential contributing factors in the development of a child who molests other children, we continue to return to the presence of some form of maltreatment or traumatic influence during the early years of these children's lives.

Community and cultural attitudes about sexual openness must be included in the discussion. Within the last fifty years we have seen a code of protective movie standards shift from an outright ban against married couples being filmed in the same bed—to the sexually explicit films of today, albeit with a rating system. The puritan modesty that left its imprint into the twentieth century was erased in the sexual revolution of the 1960s and children are exposed to a multitude of sexual stimuli long before they can comprehend or deal with what they are seeing and hearing.

We do know that children are intensely curious about their bodies at an early age. They like to touch their own bodies and the genitalia of others, if permitted. They soon learn that most adults are threatened by behavior or language that involves sexual body parts and so they create their own sexual "resource centers" on school playgrounds where whispered data is embellished, distorted, and passed on with great relish but with no accountability. Adults who shrink from sexual conversations with their sons and daughters, uncomfortable about what to say or when to say it, leave their children at the mercy of the "secret" underground. Thus, even most normal sexual behavior of children occurs at a distance from adult observation. Abnormal sexual behavior is even more covert and further removed from public countenance.

The good news is that many schools are now taking sexual harassment quite seriously and are looking for ways to effectively communicate with their students about the actions and consequences connected with harassment behavior. Some schools have been motivated by incidents on their campus, some by concern about emerging data, and some by lawsuits. One example occurred in 1994 in Minnesota. A seven-year-old girl complained of being harassed daily on her school bus by a group of young boys. The boys apparently talked of her reproductive organs and taunted her with suggestions of oral sex. Their foul language and lewd behavior frequently drove her to tears. Her mother wrote to school officials, detailing the events on the bus. The district responded by removing two students from the bus, changing seat assignments, and having school officials talk to the students. But the child's mother contended that the remedies were insufficient and she filed a sexual-harassment suit against the school district. According to reports, the school district was forced to pay a reported $15,000 for not acting on the student's behalf. Several other suits have not fared well in the courts and are under appeal at present. Beyond being sued, negligent districts also risk having federal money withheld. School boards across the country are putting sexual-harassment policies in place or adding student-to-student harassment to previous injunctions. In Essex Junction, Vermont, their policy says that harassment is "any unwanted or unwelcome sexual behavior that makes a person feel uncomfortable . . . or interferes with a person's school days." Court rulings in California and Minnesota have spurred laws requiring every elementary school and junior and senior high school to have a sexual-harassment policy. California's law covers children in the fourth grade and up, while the Minnesota law covers all children, beginning in kindergarten. The tough Minnesota law resulted in 1,000 convictions, suspensions, and expulsions during the 1991–1992 school year.

In the December 6, 1993, issue of *U.S. News and World Report*, Nan Stein, director of the Sexual Harassment in Schools Project of the Center for Research on Women at Wellesley College, says most secondary schools have policies, or are developing ones, designed to give students who feel they have been sexually harassed a way to file a formal complaint—and to give alleged harassers a mechanism allowing for a fair hearing.

Policies in conjunction with programs have the best chance of effecting substantial change. Unfortunately, very few schools have instituted educational programs to prevent the harassment from occurring in the first place. Minuteman Regional Vocational Technical High School in Lexington, MA, has one of the most widely copied sexual-harassment programs in the country. In Detroit Lakes, new seventh-grade students at the Detroit Lakes Junior High School watch a video presentation of senior high-school students acting out various scenarios, followed by on-screen discussions of whether or not sexual harassment was involved—and how. Students who were interviewed more than a month after viewing the tapes confirmed the impact and the resultant changes in language and behavior.

Peter Miner, a middle-school teacher in New York has created a Sexual Respect curriculum that has earned high praise and testimonials from his students. Miner's curriculum explores the values of his student—subjects by asking the question, "Can you espouse the values of fairness and respect, and at the same time discriminate and injure?" His lessons raise their awareness that sexist and sexually harassing behaviors are dissatisfying and, therefore, undesirable. Miner stresses that actions that alienate and hurt people are unworthy of people of intelligence and integrity. He also helps his students make a connection between the indignities of racial harassment and sexual harassment, between bigotry and sexism.

These efforts are not without criticism. Some critics complain that student to student sexual-harassment policies are an over-reaction and infringement of free speech. Albert Shanker, educator and labor leader, is concerned that the AAUW definition of sexual harassment is too broad and worries that genuine incidents of harmful harassment might be trivialized when virtually every word or gesture of a sexual nature could potentially be called sexual harassment.

On the other hand, there are those who say that verbal abuse, which has been often discounted, is now being given deserved status, at least in cases of sexual harassment. It's important to stress that noncontact sexual abuse is abusive, just as contact sexual abuse is abusive. A case of rape is certainly a greater violation than a case of sexual harassment, but we cannot ignore the latter because the former is so loathsome.

An important book on the subject of sexual harassment, *Sexual Harassment and Teens* by Susan Strauss and Pamela Espeland, tries to help students understand the differences between flattering/flirting and harmful harassment. The following chart is extracted from their material.

Sexual Harassment	Flirting
Makes the receiver feel:	
Bad	Good
Angry	Happy
Sad	Flattered
Ugly	Attractive
Powerless	In control
Results in:	
Negative self-esteem	Positive self-esteem
Is perceived as:	
One-sided	Reciprocal
Demeaning	Flattering
Invasive	Open
Degrading	Complimentary
Is:	
Unwanted	Wanted
Power-motivated	Equality-motivated
Illegal	

An article in the *Kansas City Star* by staff writer Eric Adler focused on one school's response to the problem of sexual harassment. At Harmony Middle School in suburban Kansas, the twenty-two students in a history class were asked point-blank:

"How many of you know of sexual harassment in the middle schools, in the sixth, seventh, and eighth grades?"

In a flash, the hand of every boy and girl in the room shoots into the air. "How many of you think it's harmless?" they're asked. And every hand goes down.

"How many of you think it's really damaging?" And, once again, all hands are up. One student comments: "It really lowers your self-esteem."

Asked whether they had been harassed or witnessed harassment, only a few of the eighth graders answered no. Instead, the students wrote of being pinched; boys being taunted with sexual epithets; girls having their breasts touched or brushed against, being leered at, or criticized. "People say that you're gay," wrote one student, " or I have seen boys at other schools touch girls' breasts."

"On the bus," wrote another, "there are boys in the back and they are always trying to pull the girls out of their seats and get them on the floor so they can go up their shirts and touch them and stuff."

"One time," wrote a third student, "I was just walking down the hall and I saw a boy who always grabs girls, come up behind me and he pinched my butt and grabbed it. It really bugs me a lot. I've also had boys whistling at me at swim meets when I'm about to swim."

Finally, wrote one eighth-grader: "I think it happens to 90 percent of the people in our grade."

In our conversations with students, we are continually amazed and appalled by the number of girls who express disgust with the daily onslaught of sexual harassment that includes physical, verbal, and emotional pressure. When middle-school girls are in settings where there is close proximity to male high-school students, the problem appears to be more acute.

The authors of *Sexual Harassment in Our Schools*, Robert Shoop and Jack Hayhow, are eloquent spokesmen for the cause they plead in their book. The following is an excerpt:

> Although we all wish sexual harassment was not a serious problem, whether we choose to face it or not, sexual harassment is occurring virtually every moment of every day in most every elementary and secondary schools in America. Girls are touched, commented upon, and propositioned in the public schools of every city in America. Boys comment on breasts and vaginas and make sexual requests. Some people still believe that girls secretly like this type of attention. Others think that if girls don't like it, they most certainly provoke it with their clothing, their manner of walking, or their behavior. Until recently harassment was recognized as rude, offensive, and impolite, but it was not illegal. However, the rules have changed and sexual harassment in elementary and secondary schools is now against the law.
>
> Please understand, when we talk about sexual harassment in schools, we're talking about real kids and real harm. We're talking about young people whose physical and emotional health is in grave jeopardy. And we are talking about students who feel helpless and hopeless.

In summary, sexual abuse or harassment of children by peers is strongly connected to issues of power, just as in cases where adults are involved. Similarly, the trauma for victims, at any age, is especially damaging because sexuality is so central to the core of our being and self-esteem is so profoundly affected. The most innocent taunting at an early age can have lifelong consequences.

Recommendations for consideration:

- Adults need to understand the far reaching impact of sexual harassment on children and prepare themselves to be available for advice, support, and understanding.

- Adults need to be informed about the normal sexual developmental stages that children experience.

- Adults need to help children understand what is appropriate and inappropriate behavior in public and private settings.

- Adults need to become comfortable with sexual material and establish an environment that allows for dialogue about sexual feelings, concerns, fears, etc.

- Schools should have policies regarding sexual harassment and include information and education about sexual harassment in their curriculum-at the elementary, middle, and senior high school level.

- Children need to understand that sexual abuse and harassment is a part of bullying, that it is illegal, and must be reported.

- Children need to recognize when they, and others, are abusing power in their interactions.

- Parents have the right to file a complaint with the U.S. Department of Education's Office for Civil Rights, with their state's department of education, or to bring a lawsuit under Title IX of the federal education laws.

CHAPTER SEVEN

Sibling Abuse

"I wish I didn't have any brothers or sisters."

NEARLY EVERY PARENT with more than one child has experienced the bully–victim dynamic in his or her own home. In this chapter we explore the conflicts between siblings in detail. We make a distinction between "normal" sibling conflict and sibling abuse, and give suggestions for dealing with both.

Like the peer abuse that occurs between children who are unrelated, sibling abuse can be physical, verbal, emotional, or sexual.

My two sons can be standing in the kitchen, without any evidence of tension between them, when one begins what looks like "rough-housing" with the other. Not two minutes later they can be rolling around on the floor in all-out aggressive conflict. As they become older, and stronger, I fear that one of them will be seriously injured by the other.

When I was young my brother would throw me on the floor and tickle me until I wet my pants. No matter how hard I cried and pleaded with him to let me go, he wouldn't stop. He was older and stronger than me and there was no way I could protect myself. Even when my mother knew what was going on, she wouldn't interfere. She was afraid of him, too. The abusive tickling went on for years, until he left home to go into the Navy. I've not seen or spoken to him since.

I cannot believe how cruelly and viciously my daughters can speak to each other. At times they are the best of friends, but when they are angry with each other they know how to cut to the quick with their words. The one who agonizes about her complexion is called "zit face" by the other, the one who worries about her weight is called "tub-o-lard" by the other, and so on. Most of the time the one on the receiving end tries to act like she doesn't care, but I can tell by the painful expression on her face that she tries to quickly conceal how deep these words pierce.

My older brother always left for school before I did as the older kids liked to get there early to have time to talk. Once I realized that he had forgotten his gym shoes (this was before athletic shoes were standard issue footwear for kids), and I thought I would do him a favor by bringing them to him before school started. I went to his classroom, certain that for once he would appreciate me and thank me for helping him out. He was laughing and talking with friends when someone noticed me standing at the door of the classroom and told him I was there. The expression on his face changed the instant he saw me; it was as if my very existence were the greatest humiliation he had ever experienced. He came to the door, grabbed the shoes from my hand and hissed under his breath "How could you do this to me?" I felt as if the wind had been knocked out of me.

I was sexually abused by my older brother for several years beginning at the age of five. When I was eight years old I was hospitalized for several days for a urinary tract infection, and when I returned home my parents moved me to a different bedroom, right next door to theirs, away from my old room in the basement, next door to my brother. In retrospect I think they must have known that something was going on, but they did not want to face it, or did not know how to deal with the situation. Despite the fact that my brother was very troubled, and had numerous problems in school, with teachers, and with the law, my parents always idealized him and minimized his difficulties. The abuse went on until he left home.

It is difficult to find statistics documenting the prevalence of sibling abuse. Only the more serious cases are likely to come to the attention of authorities who would keep records, yet researchers think that sibling violence occurs more frequently than parent–child or husband–wife abuse. A study by *US News & World Report* reported that 138,000 children under age seventeen used a weapon on a sibling at least once during a one-year period.

Data on verbal, emotional, and sexual abuse are hard to track because of the often fuzzy boundaries between what is "normal" teasing or conflict and abuse, and in the case of sexual abuse, experts vary in their opinions about what constitutes nonabusive sexual curiosity or exploration. Retrospective studies that ask college-age or adult women about their childhood experiences have reported that two to fifteen percent of women had had sexual experiences with siblings.[1] The same criteria that we used to identify abuse between peers who are not related are relevant here. Conflict between siblings should be considered abusive when the interaction becomes violent, when either sibling feels that he or she is powerless to stop the interaction, when the conflict persists over extended periods of time, and when the conflict is lopsided so that one sibling is singled out consistently.

Researchers suggest that sibling abuse can have damaging consequences, resulting in relationship difficulties, poor self-esteem, sexual dysfunction, depression, and other emotional problems in more chronic and severe circumstances.[2] Some of the research studies that examine sibling abuse include chaotic, disorganized families with multiple problems, which makes it difficult to generalize these findings to all families. It is also difficult to know whether the problems described are due to sibling abuse or the family's dysfunction.

Blended families often face additional challenges as step-siblings learn to live together. A second marriage may mean that a child must share a room that once was his own, or that a child who once had the role of the oldest in the family now feels displaced by her new older step-siblings.

One theme that consistently surfaces, however, in our research and experience with families is the pain many siblings felt because they did not feel their parents moved to protect them from the emotional, verbal, physical, or sexual sibling abuse that they were certain their parents observed. We know that parents can feel overwhelmed by the conflicts between their children, and incapacitated by feelings of failure when the conflicts persist. Parents *can* intervene in effective ways that can dramatically improve sibling relationships.

Adele Faber and Elaine Mazlish, authors of *Siblings Without Rivalry: How to Help Your Children Live Together So You Can Live Too*, map out many specific guidelines for dealing with sibling conflict. Throughout their book the authors return to the great discomfort parents feel witnessing cruelty between their children. It is very painful to see one child you love deeply hurt another child you also love deeply. Parents must learn to live with their discomfort and accept that negative feelings between siblings are unavoidable. Attempts to forbid negative feelings usually makes things worse. Faber and Mazlish tell us that facing and accepting the validity of these feelings is the first step to improving sibling conflict—"The very emotions that we want to close the door on and lock out need to be invited in, made welcome and treated with respect." Faber and Mazlish suggest four strategies for dealing with negative feelings toward siblings:

1. Instead of dismissing negative feelings about a sibling, acknowledge the feelings. This means that when a child makes a negative statement about a sibling, we don't try to refute the statement, or talk them out of the feeling, but instead help them put the feeling into words. When Susie tells us she hates her brother, instead of saying "No you don't—you really love him" we say "You are really angry with him."

2. *Give children in fantasy what they don't have in reality.* This means that we help our children to express the wish that underlies the negative feeling that is expressed. When Jack says that his older brother is mean because he excludes Jack from the neighborhood football game, we say "That hurts your feelings. It sounds like you wish he wanted you to play, too." This helps our children learn to identify their wants and needs, a critical step in any problem-solving process.

3. *Help children channel their hostile feelings into symbolic or creative outlets.* When Janet is upset because her sister has broken a favorite toy we help her find age-appropriate ways to express her angry feelings without fighting. This might include using a doll or stuffed animal to demonstrate her anger, drawing a picture about her feelings, or writing a letter to her sister.

4. *Stop hurtful behavior.* Show how angry feelings can be discharged safely. Refrain from attacking the attacker. When Bill is about to lash out—either verbally or physically—at his brother because he won't give Bill a turn at the computer, we stop him and describe a better way to express anger. "You seem really angry at Bill. Instead of hitting or calling names, tell him how you feel, or what you want."

Throughout their book Faber and Mazlish consistently draw a distinction between expressing feelings and acting hurtfully. It is obvious that we would be uncomfortable with hurtful actions, and many parents are equally uncomfortable with the anger and rage our children will express when given permission to do so. Some parents worry that giving children permission to express these feelings will escalate the conflict, or encourage children to act on these feelings. Just the opposite occurs, however. Allowing children to express their negative feelings consistently results in more positive interactions between siblings. Faber and Mazlish describe this paradox: "Insisting upon good feelings between the children led to bad feelings. Allowing for bad feelings between the children led to good feelings."

Parents unwittingly contribute to sibling conflict and rivalry by making comparisons between children. It is easy to see how unfavorable comparisons can generate hostility ("Stuart always helps around the house without being asked. Why do I always have to nag you to get you to do anything?"). But positive comparisons can create problems, too. When a parent tells Sharon "I wish your sister had your self-discipline. She can't seem to follow through on anything" it creates discomfort for Sharon, even though she may understand this is meant to be a compliment. Sharon may wonder if the parent feels some preference for Sharon, which may feel good in some ways, but is also likely to engender guilt, or worry about the relationship between the parent and other siblings. Faber and Mazlish encourage parents to avoid comparisons altogether. Instead, describe the behavior that you like or dislike without making any reference to other children.

Faber and Mazlish also encourage parents to avoid locking children into specific roles within the family. For example, describing Brad as "the athlete in the family" may prevent other siblings from discovering their own athletic potential, or finding that they enjoy a sport even if they are not as skilled at is as Brad. Similarly, describing Jill as "Mom's little helper" may discourage other children in the family from developing their capacity to nurture and assist because Jill appears to have the market cornered.

Parents can unwittingly lock siblings into the roles of bullies and victims, as well.

Once a particular dynamic has been established between siblings, where one child tends to pick on another, for example, it is easy to begin to see this as an immutable pattern that reflects basic elements of one or both children's personalities that cannot be changed. Once we begin to think of the situation in these terms we close the door on any other possibilities, limiting our children's development as just described in the examples of Brad and Jill. Faber and Mazlish encourage parents to respond to children in ways that do not reinforce the bully or victim role, specifically finding ways to "free the bully to be compassionate; to free the victim to be strong."

This requires that the parent work at seeing the bully's capacity for kindness, and then pointing this out to the child and the other siblings. Instead of falling into the well-worn groove of labeling and criticism ("I can't believe you could be so mean to your sister" or "You are totally selfish and think of no one but yourself"), we can set clear expectations for appropriate behavior ("I know that you can ask for what you want in a kind way" or "I expect you to be able to resolve this without using physical force").

Similarly we need to move beyond seeing the picked-on child as a helpless victim, and help the child and the other siblings see this child's potential strength. Rather than reinforcing the child's helplessness ("You poor thing! Is your brother being mean to you again?" or "Don't do that! You know how scared your sister gets."), we can respond to the child's capacity to stand up for him or herself ("You can decide for yourself whether you want to share your new toy" or "I know you can make your own scary faces if you want to, too").

It is particularly easy for the sibling with special needs—either a physical disability, emotional problems, or behavior disorder—to become cast in the role of the "problem child." Faber and Mazlish describe the dynamic that ensues: "The problem child becomes more of a problem. The burdened parents begin to make demands upon the 'normal' children to compensate for the problem child. The needs of the normal siblings are brushed aside. The normal siblings begin to resent the problem child." Faber and Mazlish suggest using similar strategies described earlier to avoid locking the child with special needs into the role of "problem child." They suggest accepting the child's frustration, rather than trying to dismiss or minimize feelings— "This isn't easy. I can tell you are frustrated" instead of "You can't help it that you have trouble with this . . . try not to think about it"; appreciating what has been accomplished, however imperfect— "You are really making progress" instead of "maybe roller skating is too difficult for you . . . let's read a book while we wait for your sister to finish"; and focusing on solutions—"This is a difficult situation. What would help?"

The relative safety and comfort of the family allows many of us to let our guard down a bit, and allow our real selves to emerge in ways that we can't in the outside world. This means that sometimes parents and siblings see cruel, deliberately vicious behavior that we would never reveal to peers. It is often painful for parents to see this side of their children—just as it is painful for parents to accept these same parts of themselves.

When we can acknowledge the aggression in our children as a natural, inevitable part of the human experience and know that this is one aspect of our child's personality, when we can see this dark side clearly and honestly and at the same time know that our child also possesses many other positive traits—then we can begin to help our children see themselves in a fuller, richer way. Just as we can panic when we see our child's deliberate acts of aggression, and in our most vulnerable moments wonder if our child is somehow evil—"the bad seed"—our children also wonder about how to feel about themselves when faced with their own anger and rage. Does the presence of such anger, even cruelty, obscure and obliterate everything that is good? Filled with shame, a child may be unable to see anything but the dark side of himself. His worst fears become a self-fulfilling prophecy as his despair about himself makes it easy to lash out at the next moment of conflict. When we can see our children at their worst, and still be able to speak to them knowing who they are at their best, we can free them to move out of the bully role. Faber and Mazlish say that we must be able to witness our children having done something monstrous without seeing them as monsters. In so doing, we can expect them to behave differently; and believe in their capacity to be kind, caring and compassionate, and most importantly, help them to believe in these, too.

Parental attitudes toward siblings and their anger can play a powerful role in reducing conflict at home. Nonetheless, some fighting is inevitable, and parents are often at a loss as to how to respond effectively. Faber and Mazlish advocate allowing siblings to resolve problems themselves for a variety of reasons. Working out their own differences helps children to become more self-sufficient and independent, and improves their problem solving skills. It also helps parents avoid making judgments without sufficient accurate information. At the same time, Faber and Mazlish advocate intervention when one child is being abused by another, or when conflict disrupts the entire household, or when a conflict continues to rage on after children have tried unsuccessfully to solve it themselves. The nature of the intervention is key, however. "We intervene, not for the purpose of settling their arguments or making a judgment, but to open the blocked channels of communication so that they can go back to dealing with each other."

Faber and Mazlish offer the following guidelines for handling different levels of fighting:

Level 1—Normal Bickering. This kind of arguing is best ignored. Parents should stay out of these conflicts to allow children practice at problem solving.

EXAMPLE

Child #1: "You're not following the rules, it's my turn"

Child #2: "No, it's not!"

Level 2—Situation Heating Up. Adult Intervention Might Be Helpful. At this point parents intervene by modeling and demonstrating basic problem solving skills, while leaving the outcome to the children. Parents can help here by acknowledging the feelings each child is having, summarizing each child's point of view, describing the problem in a way that is fair to both children, expressing confidence in the children's ability to come up with a mutually satisfying solution, and then leaving the children alone to work it out.

EXAMPLE

Child #1: "You're cheating!"

Child #2: "You're a liar."

Parent: "You both disagree with the way the other one is playing this game. It might help to go over the rules together. I know you can work this out."

Level 3—Situation Possibly Dangerous. Parents often report not knowing when children are playing or roughhousing with each other in a mutually agreeable way and when they are actually fighting. In these situations parents should ask if both children are comfortable with what is happening, and describe the guidelines for acceptable behavior (for example, roughhousing has to stop if both children are not having fun).

EXAMPLE

Child #1 begins looking over instructions, Child #2 grabs them away.

Child #1: "Let's arm wrestle to see who's right."

Child #2: (laughs) "You're on!" (Both children begin wrestling.)

Parent: "Are you both comfortable with this way of solving the problem?"

Child #1: "We're just playing, Dad."

Parent: "Wrestling is okay as long as you're both having fun."

Level 4—Situation Definitely Dangerous! Adult Intervention Necessary. When physical violence or other forms of abusive behavior are about to take place, or are already taking place, adults must intervene. Describing what you see will be instructive to the children, and help you remain calm, too—"You two both look very angry and you are hurting each other with your words." Take charge of the situation by separating the children, telling them a cooling off period is necessary. Later, when tempers have settled it may be helpful to process what happened, using the problem solving steps described in Level 2.

EXAMPLE

Child #2 pins Child #1 down. Laughter soon turns to yelling.

Child #1: "You cheated and won't admit it, let me up, you cheat!"

Child #2: "I did not, you're a rotten liar. Admit you lied, you wuss!"

Parent: "You both look very angry with each other and someone could get hurt. Stop what you're doing now' and go to your rooms until you're calm enough to work this out."

To summarize:

- Sibling abuse can be physical, verbal, emotional, or sexual.
- It is difficult to find extensive data about sibling abuse, but retrospective studies and clinical experience suggest that many people suffer significant consequences from abusive relationships with siblings. Consequences include difficulties in later relationships, poor self-esteem, sexual dysfunction, depression, and other emotional relationships.
- Some conflict between siblings is normal and unavoidable. Sibling conflict is viewed as abusive when the interaction becomes violent, when one sibling feels powerless to stop the interaction, when the conflict persists over extended periods of time, and when the conflict is lopsided so that one sibling is singled out consistently.

- Although it is difficult for parents to tolerate the negative feelings siblings can express about each other, acknowledging these feelings openly consistently results in more positive interactions between siblings.
- Parents can do much to reduce conflict between siblings by avoiding making comparisons, either positive or negative, between siblings. Teachers should also be alert to problems that result when comparisons are made between siblings.
- Similarly, parents need to guard against unwittingly locking children into set roles—such as the responsible one, the athlete, the one with a short fuse—that may limit all of the children in the family from developing to their full potential.
- Avoiding casting siblings into fixed roles of bully and victim is essential. Once this dynamic is established it maintains itself almost effortlessly, but parents can interrupt this process even after it has been up and running for years. Seeing children who bully as capable of being kind and compassionate, and seeing children who have been picked on as capable of being strong and self-reliant is the first step; expecting the corresponding behavior is the next step.
- Siblings with special needs—physical, emotional, or behavioral—can easily fall into the role of the "problem child." Parents can change their mind-set, and subsequent behavior, to alter this damaging process.
- Being able to witness children at their worst, and still hold on to the knowledge of them at their best, provides a powerful healing force.
- In general children should resolve differences on their own. When children are unable to do so, adults should intervene to open the blocked channels of

communication so that children can go back to working it out themselves. Adults also need to intervene if the conflict escalates to an abusive level, separating the children and facilitating a more effective approach later on when tempers have cooled.

NOTES

1. Finkelhor, 1979; Russell, 1983; Wyatt, 1985.
2. Wiehe, 1990; Laviola, 1989; Meiselman, 1978; Finkelhor, 1980; Graham-Bermann, 1992.

CHAPTER EIGHT

Bullies and Victims

"A victim at home can be a bully at school."

*John had been a tough, aloof loner as long as anyone could re-
member. His mother was an alcoholic and his parents divorced
when he was two years old. John was an inconvenience who had
been shuffled back and forth between them. He even spent some
time in a foster home, an experience that added to his isolation.
Although he occasionally kept company with one or two other boys,
he cared little for them and associated with them only if he could
use them for his own benefit in some way. He fought frequently
with other students at school, and the fights never seemed to be
about anything in particular. They generally started because
someone simply got on John's nerves. He never appeared anxious or
concerned when confronted about his behavior; it was as if no one
or no thing mattered enough to John to upset him. He enjoyed torturing animals, and teasing or frightening small children in the
neighborhood to the point of tears.*

*Francine transferred to a private school when she entered seventh
grade. More often than not, new students have a difficult time
finding their place in the established cliques of the day—but
Francine knew just how to work the system. She sized up the "in"
group and the "out" groups within the first week and made it her*

task to buddy up with one of the members of the most popular crowd. Before long, she was pulled into the elite circle and almost immediately took control. When Francine finished her lunch everyone at her table left when she did, even if the food was still on their plates. When Francine bought a certain kind of jeans, everyone in her group made sure they wore the same brand. If it had stopped at uneaten meals and fashion fads, Francine would never have been identified as a bully but her ambition to dominate the girls in her clique was not so easily satisfied. Francine had a very dangerous tongue. She could embellish a small fact with the art of a novelist. And sometimes she didn't wait for the fact to surface. The school rumor mill was fueled by her indefatigable desire to put down anyone who was not one of her personal devotees. Everyone was afraid of her malicious mouth and she used gossip to control her friends as well as all the "others."

Ben was a small, wiry twelve-year-old. He was constantly teased at school because of his size and limited social skills. He hated being short and was bitter about the fact that he had no friends his own age. Ben either hung around a few nineteen-year-old males he admired because they were tough troublemakers who were not intimidated by anyone, or spent time with two boys several years younger with whom he could adopt an air of bravado and self-confidence. Ben began getting in fights at school, taking on other smaller adolescents whom he had a chance of overpowering. Ben wanted to be well liked by peers, but he did not know how to make friends. Ben was creative and imaginative, and wrote science-fiction stories with strong heroic figures, who matched Ben's own hypervigilance to any injustice in his environment. He jumped at the opportunity to start a fight with anyone who made cruel remarks about another child who was weaker or smaller. He saw himself as a champion of the defenseless and justified his attacks with the conviction that he was a noble defender. He had no idea that he was a bully.

*Roland was pudgy. His classmates teased him about his "beer belly."
Because he had no waistline they would refer to him as a pickle.
Their taunts did not seem to bother him. You might have even
thought that he thrived on the attention. He was a lightning rod for
any excess energy in the classroom. He was unkempt and his hair was
never combed. Some days he would start screaming during class for
no apparent reason, but his favorite modus operandi was to gross out
his fellow students. One of his signature tricks was to lift up his shirt,
extend his stomach as much as he could, and expose his belly button
to anyone in sight. On one occasion, when he had a runny nose, he
wiped the mucus with his hands and then attempted to smear it on
the clothing of his classmates.*

We have given a brief description of four bullies. It is reported that one in four bullies will end up in the criminal correc-
tion system. One of these four did. Which one would you predict
would get in trouble with the law?

John, Francine, Ben, and Roland would all be easily identified as bullies; Ben and Roland also had experience as victims of
aggressors. In this chapter we explore the characteristics of bullies
and victims, and look at the ways that the roles of bully and victim
overlap for some children. We review what researchers are telling
us about who bullies and victims are, and how they come to play
those roles. We share what we have learned from talking to students in school about their experience, and raise some of the areas
of disagreement in the field.

WHAT WE KNOW ABOUT BULLIES
Bullies Come in Different Forms
John and Ben represent different kinds of bullies who share the
common characteristic of fighting with other children, but differ
in several important ways. Psychologists Kenneth Dodge, Ph.D.,
and John Coie, Ph.D., have described two different styles of ag-

gression in their research with children—**reactive** and **proactive**.[1] The **reactive** aggressive child is emotional, has poor impulse control, and reacts to an accidental bump as an act of provocation. This child feels constantly threatened and thus believes that his aggressive response is justified. Some researchers suggest that this form of aggression is the most violent.[2] Ben would be described as reactively aggressive according to this classification system.

Proactive aggressive children differ in that they behave in a non-emotional, controlled, deliberate manner. The aggression is delivered with the hope of achieving some goal that comes from *within* the aggressive child, like coercion or domination, rather than in response to some external threat. John would be described as a proactive bully from this perspective.

Bullies Are Cultivated

Returning to our concentric circles, some children are more likely to become bullies because of inborn traits like distractibility. The number of children diagnosed as Attention Deficit Hyperactive Disorder (ADHD) is increasing, many of whom are identified as bullies because of their disruptive behavior. According to experts 2,000,000 children are known to be taking the medication Ritalin because of ADHD.[3] Ritalin makes it possible for these children to accommodate to the classroom environment, control their actions and interactions, and contain bullying behavior.

Most researchers agree, however, that bullies generally become bullies through their *life experiences*, as opposed to being *born* bullies. Bullies frequently share certain experiences in their families or communities. For example, bullies are more likely to *have been abused* themselves than kids who are not bullies. Nathaniel Floyd, Ph.D., a psychologist in Westchester County, New York, says that the experience of having been a victim at home often makes a child more likely to be a bully at school. Dr. Floyd says that seeing other children who appear vulnerable is uncomfortable for the bully. "When these bullies see kids they perceive as vulnerable, they are threatened because it reminds them of the shame and humiliation of their own victimization."[4]

We see evidence of this pattern in our discussions with students. We have been surprised by the number of students who have expressed contempt for students who did not stand up for themselves. There are several possible explanations for these students' reaction. Perhaps these students would not tolerate being a victim and are impatient with those who do. Or perhaps it disturbs them to see a bully inherit undeserved power. Or perhaps they are uncomfortable observing the victim's pain and resent the idea that they might have to take responsibility to intervene, or feel guilty about their inability to do so. Or, as Floyd suggests, perhaps they identify with the victim, and feel ashamed and humiliated by their own history of exploitation.

Bullies are more likely to have *witnessed their fathers physically abusing their mothers, or have seen other forms of violence in their homes*. A large body of psychological research has demonstrated that viewing violent behavior is more likely to lead to acting violently. This was true for Ben who listened and watched in horror as his mother was slapped and beaten by his father. Leonard Eron, Ph.D., and Rowell Huesmann, Ph.D., at the University of Illinois–Chicago have been following a large group of students for the past thirty years. They say that there are three ideal conditions for learning aggressive behavior: watching others act aggressively, including viewing aggression on television; being rewarded for acting aggressively; and being treated aggressively. These researchers say the patterns for aggressive behavior are already well established by the age of eight.

Certain *parenting styles* are seen more frequently in the families of children who are bullies. Dr. Eron says bullies are more likely to have parents who ignore their children, who are unaware of what is happening in the lives of their children, and who use harsh and inconsistent discipline strategies. In John's family, financial pressures and marriage problems preoccupied both parents, and they often were unaware of John's concerns and problems. John and his younger siblings argued with each other constantly. Although both parents disliked the arguing, most of the time they tried to ignore it. When one of the parents was having a particularly difficult day, however, they might explode, issuing severe penalties for the bickering like permanently taking away John's new bike that had been a birthday gift, or refusing to allow him to go on a camping trip he had been eagerly awaiting for weeks. In both cases the punishment did not seem to fit the crime, and the usual tolerance of the similar behavior made the harsh punishment even more difficult to understand. Parents of bullies are also more likely to use physical discipline measures like spanking or hitting.

Gerald Patterson, Ph.D., a psychologist in Eugene, Oregon, reported in his research results that parents of aggressive children discipline their children based on the parents' mood, rather than on the behavior of the child. This means that behavior that might be punished when a parent is in a bad mood might also be tolerated without any consequences if the parent is in a good mood. Although every parent has probably responded in this fashion on occasion, recurrent use of this kind of inconsistent discipline is likely to leave a child confused about what constitutes appropriate behavior.

Dan Olweus, Ph.D., a psychologist in Norway and one of the earliest researchers in this field, describes similar family dynamics. "Too little love and care and too much freedom in childhood . . . contribute strongly to the development of an aggressive behavior."[5] According to his research, parents of bullies are more likely to have little time to spend with their children, leaving their children without a sense of being loved and cared for, and without clear guidelines for appropriate behavior. Francine came from a wealthy family who had indulged her with extravagant gifts but had little time to give her the warmth and concern she craved.

Bullies' Thinking Patterns Are Distorted
A number of researchers have investigated the cognitive processes or thinking patterns of bullies. Dodge and Coie have found that

reactively aggressive children (but not proactively aggressive chil-dren) tend to presume that others have hostile intentions toward them. Dr. Dodge describes reactively aggressive children as seeing the world through a paranoid lens. "They see threats where none exist, and they take these imagined threats as provo-cations to strike back." These errors in thinking are well in place by the age of seven or eight. An innocent brush is viewed as a bla-tant attack, which Dodge says allows the child to "feel justified in retaliating for what actually are imaginary harms."[6]

John Lochman, Ph.D., makes related observations about bullies. He reports that bullies consistently see other children as more aggressive than themselves. "Bullies see their anger as justi-fied. They see the other kid as having started the trouble."[7]

Robert Selman, Ph.D., has examined another aspect of the thinking patterns of bullies. He focuses on the immaturity of bul-lies' cognitive style, describing it as *unilateral* in nature. These chil-dren think in terms of simple one-way directives and commands to others—"Give that to me," for example. They lack a more mature form of thinking that allows for a reciprocal exchange of ideas and collaboration and, as a result, enable people to effectively resolve differences with each other. Selman and his colleagues suggest that the bully has limited skills to manage relationship conflicts, and this, in turn leads to anger and aggression.

Bullies Often Grow Up to Be Criminals
Dr. Eron and his colleagues at the University of Chicago have been following the lives of a large group of bullies for over thirty years, and their findings are sobering. By age thirty, 25 percent of the adults who had been identified as bullies as children had a criminal record, as opposed to 5 percent of the adults who had not been bullies as children. They were more likely to have dropped out of school, and to be working in a job below their skill level. They were more likely to be abusive toward their wives, and to punish their children with harsh physical discipline. It is not surprising, then, that the children of these adults were also

more likely to be bullies. Dr. Eron's research shows that bullies' traits can be traced over three generations.[8] This important research makes it clear that bullying is not only a serious problem in the lives of school children, but also a significant social problem in the larger culture.

Chris was a bully. Chris is presently an inmate at the Lansing Correctional Facility in Lansing, Kansas. To help us shed light on this problem, Chris consented to be interviewed in December 1995.

Question: At what age did you become a bully?

Answer: I believe that I became a bully at the age of three or four. I would try to control my parents through screaming or breaking things. I did that to get my way—to stop them from going out and leaving me with a babysitter. I do believe I became a bully toward my peers at eight years old. I remember punching my friend in the stomach when he didn't want to share his *Star Wars* toys.

Question: Had you been a victim before you were a peer bully?

Answer: I think I got the idea of using anger to get your way from watching my parents argue and break things. When I started to bully my peers I believe it was because how I felt when another kid my age (about eight) beat me up pretty good. I remember feeling pretty powerless.

Question: What was your motivation—attention, power, status, control, a way to express anger, a challenge to see if you could get away with it?

Answer: My motivation was to cover inadequacies such as I am not good looking, and I'm small in build compared to others my age. I also did it to cure low self-esteem following when someone else bullied me. When I was in about the seventh grade I refused to be a victim any longer. I started bullying the bullies and carrying weapons.

Question: What kind of feelings did you have when you bullied someone?

Answer: Powerful, in control, false happiness, respected, feared.

Question: Were there ever any consequences?

Answer: I was suspended from school several times and finally expelled. I was also grounded several times. I went to jail for physically assaulting people on a few occasions.

Question: How long did you remain a bully?

Answer: I remained a bully up until one year before I became incarcerated when I was nineteen.

Question: Do you see any correlation between being a bully and becoming a criminal?

Answer: Yes, I felt I had to live up to the reputation everyone gave me. So eventually I wasn't afraid of committing any crime. I felt invincible, that everyone feared me, and I could get away with anything.

Question: Do you recall any of your victims?

Answer: Every day I think of them. I wonder how what I did to them affects them. How I could have done those things. I think to them I must be a monster.

Question: Did other kids encourage you to become a bully?

Answer: Yes. The more things I did the more people wanted to hang around me. I believe they hung around me to avoid becoming a target of my aggression. Also it made them appear powerful to other people.

Question: Would you say your bullying took the form of physical, verbal, emotional, or sexual abuse?

Answer: Mostly it took the form of verbal and physical abuse. I would usually try to verbally attack someone to get them to fear me.

Question: Did any adult ever make an effort to get you to stop being a bully?

Answer: There were several attempts at stopping my bullying behavior. My teachers at school tried to stop my bullying as did my mother and father. I can't say any of it made a great difference because I did not want to change. The person I can say that came the closest was my mother. She would try to communicate with me but I would shut down. I would also fake change to get people to leave me alone.

Question: As you look back, do you think there is anything that anyone could have done to change the course your life has taken?

Answer: I believe the only thing that would have helped me then would have been teaching me about self-esteem and empathy and constant reinforcement of those ideals.

Gender Differences in Bullying

Although we might tend to think of bullies as boys, girls are also bullies, too, as Francine's case illustrates. Researchers report that boy bullies are three or four times more likely to be physically aggressive than girl bullies. Girls are more likely to bully other girls by ostracizing or ignoring, or manipulating psychologically through peer pressure. One student we spoke to described this as "mind games." This gender difference may be shifting slightly, however, as in our work we hear more frequent reports of physical confrontations between girls.

John was the bully who ended up in prison. His vicious and cruel behavior escalated, leading to arrests for breaking and entering by late middle school, and armed robbery by the end of high school. John's early adulthood was spent moving in and out of correctional facilities for a series of increasingly violent crimes.

Francine continued to dominate her classmates all through high school. The verbal and emotional abuse she imposed on others was never seriously challenged by adults or peers. We can only wonder about the quality of her relationships as an adult, and the impact her abuse had on her victims.

Ben was fortunate to be in a school that adopted a peer mediation program. Ben went through the training and became an excellent mediator. His empathy for his mother and the victims he defended in school worked to his advantage in a peer counseling role. In the process of mediating conflicts between other students and honing his ability to listen to their disputes he earned the respect he had always coveted.

It took a few years, but Roland was eventually recognized as a child who was being sexually abused by his stepfather. His disruptive and inappropriate behavior ended up mobilizing concerned adults in his environment, which allowed Roland to receive the help he needed. In fourth grade Roland ended up in the classroom of a loving teacher who talked and talked and talked to Roland alone, to his classmates without Roland present, and to Roland and his classmates together. She held several meetings with his family but these conferences did not alter the situation. When he had outbursts in class she developed a network of other school personnel such as the school counselor, the nurse, and a caring custodian who could spend time with him until he calmed down. When the information about his sexual abuse finally surfaced he was transferred to a classroom specifically designed for children with behavior disorders. He is now working with a trained specialist, in a one-to-one relationship, and at last update is doing better.

WHAT WE KNOW ABOUT VICTIMS

Angela is slight eleven-year-old girl who looks younger than most of her classmates. She walks with a slight limp because of a mild birth defect. She is self-conscious, quiet, and reserved at school, often going through the entire day without saying more than a few words to anyone. Although she is in the gifted program in her school and very talented musically, these assets give her little confidence with her peers. Every day Angela dreads music class, where she has to sit next to a boy who taunts her under his breath for the entire class period. Some times other children sitting nearby hear the degrading names he calls her, names that have no apparent connection to Angela and do not even refer to her disability, but most of the time Angela is the only audience for his teasing. Either way the humiliation is unbearable for her. She imagines that the other children must feel the same abhorrence for her. She says nothing when he teases her, trying to act as if she did not hear him, which is nearly impossible when she knows others have heard. She does not know how to get him to stop. Once music class is over Angela does not have to have any other close contact with this boy, and, fortunately, no one else usually bothers her. Still, this thirty-minute period each day affects her entire school experience, leaving her full of shame and self-doubt. When Angela thinks about the situation objectively, she knows she has much more going for her than the boy next to her, who barely makes passing grades and is frequently in trouble with teachers, but this knowledge provides no consolation for her. She tells no one of her distress, and tries to wall herself off from him and other students, almost all of whom seem like potential tormentors. At home, around familiar adults, Angela is more relaxed, and her intellect and sense of humor are more evident. Still, she frequently cries herself to sleep as she thinks about facing another day of loneliness and torment. Her parents are unaware of her distress, as are her teachers who mistake her social isolation for shyness.

Willy is a ten-year-old boy with a short fuse and quick temper. Other kids know that he is easily angered, and enjoy provoking him just to get a rise out of him. Most often, though, Willy initiates his own conflicts by hitting and pushing others, making fun of others, and getting others into trouble. He fights frequently with many kids, but he is especially adept at aggravating one particularly tough bully in the school. Willy tries to trip this boy in the hall, or take a ball away from him at recess. Often these provocations end up in a physical fight where Willy gets hurt, but he continues to go after this bully.

Victims Come in Different Forms, Too

Just as researchers have identified different subtypes of bullies, they also identify two kinds of victims. One group, identified as *low-aggressive* by David Perry, Ph.D., and colleagues and *passive* by Olweus, are described as anxious and insecure.[9] This group of students appear to do nothing to invite the bully's aggression, and also do not attempt to defend themselves when attacked. Angela fits the description of the passive victim perfectly. She has never done anything to provoke her tormentor, and is so incapacitated by the humiliation she feels that she does not know how to defend herself or try and stop the bullying behavior.

The second group, called *high-aggressive* by Perry and *provocative* by Olweus, are described as hot-tempered and restless. These victims create tension by irritating and teasing others, and are more likely to fight back when they are attacked. Willy is a provocative victim. At times Willy can be mistaken for a bully, because he initiates the conflict, but he is no match for the bully he takes on and inevitably loses in the confrontation. Provocative victims may have Attention Deficit Hyperactive Disorder or learning disabilities that prevent them from picking up on social cues other children intuitively understand.

Other children and adults describe provocative and aggressive victims as argumentative, disruptive, inattentive, and physically aggressive. Like Willy, these children are irritating to others without even realizing it. These children are not good at reading the signals that other children give and misjudge how other children see them.

Perry and his colleagues, who have studied victims extensively, say that other non-victimized children describe victims as consistently having three qualities that may make them vulnerable to bullies. Victims are:

1. More likely to "reward" their bullies with tangible resources, like giving over lunch money when it is demanded, or giving up the ball they are playing with at recess.
2. Victims are more likely to show distress, to let the bully know that he or she is getting to the victim. Some children see this as the intangible "reward" as opposed to the child who deprives the bully of the

gratification of understanding how powerful he or she is by acting indifferent.

3. Victims are less likely to punish the bully by retaliation.

Gary Ladd, Ph.D., a psychologist in Illinois, also thinks there is some kind of signal system that connects bullies to certain victims. He suggests that bullies do not pick on others at random, but instead engage in a "shopping process" to find the victims that will become their preferred targets. While over half of all children report being victimized at least once a year, and about 22 percent of students report being victimized frequently at the beginning of the school year, by the end of the year only eight percent of students report being regularly subjected to a bully's attacks.[10] Ladd thinks that some kind of vulnerability revealed in the school environment increases the likelihood of being picked on frequently. The children we talk with in schools tell us that even the infrequent experiences of victimization can be very distressing, and those who become the frequent targets of bullies suffer greatly.

There is some disagreement about whether specific physical characteristics make children more vulnerable to bullying, like wearing glasses, being overweight, or having a disability. Several researchers say they find no objective data to support the idea that these kinds of traits set a child up to be bullied, and instead report that the child's personality style makes the important difference. These investigators report that victims are more likely to be anxious, insecure children who are socially unskilled and do not stand up to their bullies.

The children we meet through our work disagree with this position. They report that children with specific disabilities, or any deviation from the norm, are primary targets for bullies. They point out that verbal taunts aimed at victims often specifically refer to a victim's physical characteristics.

On the other hand, not all children with disabilities or physical differences are victims of bullying. This suggests that personality variables do play an important role, perhaps determining which physically vulnerable children end up being victims. Perhaps the disability itself is not what makes these children vulnerable to bullying, but rather their insecure and anxious posture, which may have developed in response to the disability. While Angela's bully never directly mentioned her physical disability, her acute sense of being different, her profound sense of deformity contributed to her insecurity which may, in turn, have made her a target for bullying.

We also find that some children are victimized because they are talented, bright, or popular. They do not fit the category of either the passive or the provocative victim. A perfect example is the case of Damon. Damon was academically gifted and paid the price for being smart at his inner city middle school. The social value in that particular school was "doggin' " or "dissin'." Students got points from their peers when they showed disrespect to someone in authority. Anyone who tried to please a teacher by doing homework, extra assignments, or speaking up in class was belittled and ostracized. Damon was torn between his desire to go to college and his wish to be liked. When he concentrated on his education, he suffered the scorn of his peers. During seventh grade he gave into the peer pressure and refrained from trying to make good grades. But in his eighth grade year he reversed his decision and chose to absorb the abuse rather than sacrifice his goals. When he graduated from middle school he enrolled in a college preparatory magnet high school where achievement was the social norm and he was no longer bullied for having dreams. Damon is now attending Yale University on a scholarship, but he feels sorry for so many of his friends who could not find the strength to endure the teasing and abandoned their opportunities.

Long-Term Consequences for Victims

Like bullies, victims are more likely to have difficulties later in life. Children who were bullied in early grade school are more likely to have difficulty adjusting to middle school, are more likely to have academic difficulties, and are more likely to drop out of school.[11] Girls who are bullied are more prone to depression.[12] Patterson and his colleagues in Oregon found that students who are rejected by their peers at age ten are more likely to associate with troublemaking children at age twelve.[13] One researcher suggests that some boys who are frequently victimized by bullies develop such discomfort with the opposite sex that they find it difficult to date and marry in future years.[14] Although the scars that victims carry may be less visible than the host of problems experienced by bullies in later life, it is clear from our adult survey that the pain runs deep.

The case of Nathan Faris, described in Chapter One, calls into question the issue of teen suicide. In Japan in November 1994, a student who hanged himself left a suicide note that described years of torment by four classmates who teased him, beat him, immersed his head in a river, and extorted over $10,000 from him, most of which he had stolen from his parents. Shortly thereafter, three other teenagers who had also been bullied also hanged themselves. More recently a thirteen-year-old boy who hanged himself left a poignant suicide note. He identified his tormentors and wrote: "I've been bullied. They've taken my money. I will sacrifice myself. Please save other children."

We might assume that teen problems in Japan are much different than teen problems in the U.S. Unfortunately, this is not the case. The National Center for Health Statistics reported that suicide rates for those from fifteen to nineteen years old in our country edged up from 1,797 in 1980 to 2,009 in 1989. Experts estimate that ten times that number in the age group attempt suicide.

In Goffstown, New Hampshire, a teen suicide in October 1993 brought the town to the painful realization that five teens in the picturesque rural community of 15,000 residents had ended their lives over a two-and-a-half-year period. The last victim, who shot herself, left a note saying she could no longer endure harassment by a clique of classmates.

As anguished students and adults tried to understand what was causing their town to have a youth suicide rate 40 percent above the national average of 12 per 100,000, some people focused on 'teens' hazing, harassment and violence," according to an article by John Larrabee in the October 22, 1993, issue of *USA Today.*

"High school cliques have been around forever, but not like this," says parent Doris Danbois. "If kids don't wear brand names on their behinds, they get picked on. If you're the one who gets singled out, there's no limit to how low your self-esteem can go."

Family and friends of Megan Pauly, a sophomore at the 900-student regional high school, says she was a target. "This child was so traumatized that she thought this was the only way out," says her aunt, Bonnie Catoni. Her mother Pauline Pauly Kinduris says Megan was tormented by three girls who used to be her friends. Kinduris says her daughter once called home for a ride last year because she was afraid to walk alone. While picking up Megan Kinduris saw the group and asked, "Why can't you leave my daughter alone?" The girls responded with curses and catcalls. In her suicide note Megan said she'd been beaten up and threatened with harm if she returned to school. These tragic examples must serve as a call to action, urging us to actively intervene in the lives of these young people who are in such pain.

Interventions for Bullies and Victims

A variety of strategies are being used to intervene in bully–victim conflicts in schools around the world. Many approaches target a specific bully or victim group. Most of the interventions aimed at the proactive bully, the child like John who is calm and deliberate in his bullying, and does not appear to be very attached to anyone, are aimed at changing the *setting*, rather than the child. Some of these interventions that deal primarily with creating an environment that does not tolerate bullying have been very effective. This might include increasing adult supervision during unstructured activities like lunch or recess, and in the more remote parts of the building where bullying is most likely to occur. These kinds of interventions often include raising awareness on the part of the staff and students about what constitutes bullying, and developing clear and consistent consequences for aggressive behavior.

Programs dealing with the reactive bully like Ben take a different approach, and focus instead on changing the child, by helping the bully to alter the distorted thinking patterns that make aggression seem justified. Learning to look at other's behavior more objectively, increasing the capacity for understanding someone else's feelings, and learning to express anger and frustration are key components of approaches used with the reactive bully. The peer mediation program was the perfect answer for Ben.

Interventions aimed at the provocative victim focus on decreasing the socially inappropriate behaviors of kids like Willy. This might include an evaluation for attention deficit hyperactivity disorder (and medication, if appropriate), impulse-control strategies, and the kind of anger-management training that is used with the reactive bully. Interventions aimed at increasing the awareness of how behavior is perceived by others would be used with this victim group, too.

Passive victims benefit from approaches aimed at increasing their self-esteem and social confidence. These kind of interventions generally include assertiveness training, social skills rehearsal, and role play. Helping these children identify their special gifts and appreciate their skills is an important part of this approach.

In Chapter Eleven we will discuss a number of specific classroom interventions that have proven successful for many adults and children.

SUMMARY

Researchers have identified two types of bullies—proactive and reactive—and two types of victims—passive and provocative.

We believe there is a third type of victim who is powerful in some way and poses a threat to those who lack personal power. Just because these victims have a positive self-concept does not mean they are unaffected by cruel attacks by peers.

Certain interventions have better results with different types of bullies and victims. Strategies range from therapy and counseling to structure and consequences. Skill training in conflict resolution, anger management, assertiveness, self-esteem, and social interaction can benefit bullies and victims.

Returning to our concentric circles, it becomes clear that the personality and physiology of the individual is a significant influence. Certain qualities and characteristics predispose certain children to bully or be victimized.

The family experience regarding attachment, nurturing, discipline, conflict, neglect, and violence is quite influential in the cases we have described. The quality of relationships in the early years of development set the stage for all later relationships, affecting a child's place in the complex pattern of connections with teachers, classmates, and authority figures.

The school is a particularly powerful influence. A school that draws clear boundaries to guarantee personal safety and offers a range of programs to support student harmony can help keep student aggression in check. A school that ignores and tolerates bullying inevitably shifts the power from the adults to the peer perpetrators.

The community needs to weigh in on the side of the child. Neighbors and norms can provide some of the structure that family and school will not or cannot. In the case of the proactive bully John, the community could have made a difference when John was temporarily removed from his home. The right foster parent, a concerned case worker, a sensitive employer— any of these could have been a powerful catalyst for change. Abused and neglected children who survive and succeed invariably maintain that one adult who believed in them made the difference in their lives.

Cultural attitudes about the value of education, respect for authority, media influences, alcohol, and drug abuse play an enormous role in the lives—and outcomes—of bullies and victims. Remember Dr. Eron's research that classified viewing violence on television as influential as witnessing violence in the home. We know that cultural influences are as powerful as they are pervasive, and yet the extent to which they are embedded in our lives makes it difficult to step back and observe their power in action.

We have explored the dimensions of bullying, and the various types and characteristics of bullies and victims. In the next chapter we will examine ways to help children deal more effectively with bullying.

NOTES

1. Dodge, K.A. & Coie, J.D. (1987). Social information-processing factors in reactive and proactive agression in children's peer groops. *Journal of Personality and Social Psychology*, 53, 1146-1158.

2. Lorenz, K. (1966). *On Aggression*. New York: Harcourt, Brace & World.

3. Breggin, P.R. & Barkley, R. (1995). Q: are behavior-modifying drugs overprescribed for America's school children? *Insight on the News*, 11, 18-22.

4. NSSC Resource paper: School Bullying and Victimization. (1995). Malibu, CA: National School Safety Center, p. 5.

5. Roberts, Marjory. (1988) Schoolyard Menace. *Psychology Today*.

6. NSSC Resource paper, p. 3.

7. NSSC Resource paper, p. 3.

8. Goleman, Daniel. (1987). The bully: New research depicts a paranoid, lifelong loser. *The New York Times*, April 7.

9. Perry, D.G., Kusel, S.J., & Perry, L.C. (1988). Victims of peer aggression. *Developmental Psychology*, 24, 807-814; Olweus, D. (1978). *Aggression in the Schools: Bullies and Whipping Boys*. Washington, D.C.: Hemisphere.

10. Marano, H.E. (1995). Big Bad Bully. *Psychology Today*, 50, 50-68.

11. Parker, J.G. & Asher, S.R. (1987). Peer relations and later personal adjustment: Are low-accepted children at risk? *Psychological Bulletin*, 103, 357-389.

12. Kupersmidt, J.B. & Patterson, C.J. (1991). Childhood peer rejection, aggression, withdrawal and perceived competence as predictors of self-re-

ported behavior problems in preadolescence. *Journal of Abnormal Child Psychology*, 19, 427-449.

13. Patterson, G. R., Capaldi, D., & Bank, L. (1991). An early starter model for prediction delinquency. In D. Pepler & K. H. Rubin (Eds.), *The Development and Treatment of Childhood Aggression*. Hillsdale, NJ: Erlbaum.

14. Gilmartin, B.G. (1987). Peer group antecedents of severe love-shyness in males. *Journal of Personality*, 55, 467-489.

CHAPTER NINE

Empowering Children

"It's hard to stop teasing."

BULLYING WILL NEVER be eliminated unless adults and children become partners in this crusade against cruelty.

In this chapter, we will focus on the role that students can play. Empowering young people to deal with this problem themselves is crucial. For one thing, many bullying incidents are hidden from adults and occur outside of their awareness. For another, young people are often reluctant to report incidents to parents or teachers for fear of retaliation. But a more compelling reason is that children are the experts on this subject and we must find a way to bring them into the discussion. When I meet with young people I implore them to teach me all they know. Their response has been invaluable and confirmed our belief in the seriousness of the problem.

The younger the child, the more likely he or she is to seek help from an authority. By the time children reach middle school, where the problems are most intense, they are less likely to reach out for adult intervention. It is at this stage that young people feel most trapped, most isolated, and most helpless to deal with the pressure.

There are many children who will never be able to thwart a bully by themselves and in those cases it is imperative that an adult step in to ensure protection.

There are other cases, however, when children can be key players in bringing about change. Bullies, victims, and witnesses all have an important role to play.

When I approach students about the issue of peer abuse, I usually begin by confessing that adults have much to learn about solving today's problems, especially about bullying.

When I ask students the question "Why does someone become a bully?" they are amazingly perceptive about the psychological connections between the cause and effect of bullying behavior.

A typical series of responses will be: "They want attention," "They want power," "They don't have confidence in themselves," "Is jealous of someone who has something he or she can't have," "Don't know how to control their anger," "They may be getting abused at home and take it out on us," "Doesn't know how to get what they want in an appropriate way," "Lacks self-esteem," "Was a victim and now wants revenge," "They're just mean and evil," "They like to have people be afraid of them," "They pick on someone before someone can pick on them," "When they were born, their parents didn't teach them how to be nice," "They want to be popular." One student even raised his hand to claim that "being a bully is fun!"

The bully as "popular" puzzled me but it was mentioned too many times to be discounted. I would always ask why someone who is mean would be popular. One day, a slight sixth grader posed the question this way: "I would like to ask the girls why they would rather hang around with the tough guys than boys who are nicer."

I suggested to the girls that such behavior might be sending a wrong message, might encourage bullies to continue their troublesome ways. If curbing bullies is a goal, we deserved an explanation. A young girl stood up and said that when girls don't feel safe, they look to a bully to protect them.

The importance of this kind of open discussion is to expose the bully's weakness. A bully's power can be deflated when he or she is publicly revealed as someone who lacks self-esteem, craves attention, is abused at home. Students who would never have the courage to confront a bully alone are bolstered to make pointed observations when they are part of a group discussion about bullies. Reducing the bully's power is essential, not only for the sake of the victim, but because today's bullies can become tomorrow's criminals if we don't help them set limits on their aggression. Surely our society has something more to offer our disruptive children than to wait for their incarceration.

Students are equally insightful when asked "Why does someone become a victim?" Their replies are: "Because they're different," "They're not cool," "Too smart," "Too dumb," "Don't stick up for themselves," "Too shy," "Has a physical problem," "Too popular," "Wear glasses or braces," "Their skin is a different color," "Too tall or too short," "Won't fight back," "They're teacher's pet," "Not good in sports," "They wear funny clothes," "Just don't like 'em," "They pick on other kids, so we pick on them," "They cry real easy."

Reaching out to work with the victims is terribly important because their withdrawal can lead to social scars, depression, and possible suicide. According to the Center for Disease Control and Prevention, children aged ten to fourteen committted suicide twice as often in the 1990s as they did in the 1980s. Some victims retaliate, become the aggressor, and ultimately end up as bullies. Victims need an opportunity to give a voice to their pain. Invariably, one child will disclose the fact that he or she has been bullied which gives others a chance to expand their capacity for empathy. On some occasions, bullies have even come forward and apologized for their mistreatment.

I will always remember Chris. Toward the end of a discussion about bullies and victims at an elementary school in suburban St. Louis on a cold February morning, a tentative young girl came up to the microphone and revealed she had been teased a lot. She said it really bothered her, that sometimes the boys made her cry, and crying makes her feel embarrassed. Nothing in our discussion had riveted the audience quite like this plaintive appeal. I'm not sure whether it was her courage, her eloquence, or her pain that resulted in her bully, a young man named Chris, standing up to apologize to her in front of the assembled fourth- and fifth-graders. A gasp went up from teachers as well as students and I invited Chris to come to the front of the room to receive our gratitude and praise. I could tell that this was not the first time Chris had been singled out in the presence of his peers but I doubted that he had ever been greeted by such a collection of admiring faces and warm applause. I was so moved by Chris's confession, I sent him a valentine the next week and received the following reply;

> *Dear Mrs. Fried,*
> *Thank you for the valentine. It's hard to stop teasing.*
> *I think that it would be nice if you come back next year.*
> *I am working on trying not to tease. Ceep* [sic] *talking to boys and girls about teasing.*
> *Chris*

Though there is conflicting data about the percentage of children who are identified as victims, the majority of students in a given classroom are neither bullies nor victims, they are witnesses to the bullying. These students need to understand the power they have to effect change. Witnesses must be recruited, not only because they can be such powerful change agents, but also because of the price they pay for witnessing cruelty. Children who are spectators in the arena of bullying will not be unscathed. The conflict they experience can lead to feelings of sadness, anger, guilt, and shame. If they support the bully, they are an accomplice to the crime; if they stand up for the victim, they are at risk to become the next target; if they remain silent, they may carry a burden of guilt for many years.

An example of this is a memory shared by a colleague of mine who is an esteemed, successful professional in the child-advocacy field.

Andrew was a popular student. He excelled in academics and athletics and was a respected school leader. A beleaguered young girl, Becky, in his sixth-grade class was selected for ridicule on a daily basis because of her lesser socioeconomic position. Her clothing, vocabulary, and lack of social skills set her apart and the children composed a song about her deficiencies, which they gleefully sang to her every morning.

Many years have past since Andrew's elementary school experiences but he is constantly reminded of Becky's grief when he meets someone who has her name or her facial characteristics. Andrew claims there is a wound in his soul that will never heal when he thinks about his vulnerable schoolmate. In retrospect, he believes he should have stopped the assaults though he had neither the skills nor the authority to counter the fervor of his sanctimonious peers. He wonders if Becky became a casualty of the schoolyard battlefield, a wounded veteran who never recovered from the wars of recess. He also thinks about the bully who was the ringleader of this campaign. Did he ever find a constructive way to acquire power or did he finally meet his match at the hands of someone more cruel than he? But mostly he thinks about the missed chance to make a difference in both of their lives.

I am always impressed with the wisdom that surfaces when children are asked to come up with ideas for bullies, victims, and bystanders. Some of the best suggestions come when there is an opportunity to break into small groups for brainstorming sessions. The following opinions have been collected over several years.

What can a bully do?

Learn how to handle your anger.

Ask yourself: "Why am I doing this?"

Get help to feel better about yourself.

Try to stop picking on someone for just one day.

Listen to a friend.

Talk to another bully and discuss your behavior.

Form a "Bullies Anonymous" group.

Experience some consequences.

Recognize what you are doing.

Work really hard to control your behavior.

Think about how you would feel if you were the victim.

Try to get attention by doing something good.

What can a victim do?

Ignore the bully.

Walk away.

Use humor.

Think about good things.

Talk to a friend.

Tell an adult.

Stand up for yourself.

Get involved in some activities that make you feel good.

Threaten a bully who might back-off from strength.

Use "I" messages.

Involve a peer mediator.

Take karate lessons.

Fight back as a last resort.

Share your feelings.

Try to make a friend of the bully.

Go to another school.

Give the bully a compliment.

Give the bully a hug.

Some of these suggestions provoked further discussion. For instance, one student observed that if you tell someone "I don't like what you are doing to me, please stop" it could make it worse. "If you don't like the student and you have no feeling for him, you're not going to stop just because they ask you to."

Stick Up For Yourself! Every Kid's Guide to Personal Power and Self-Esteem by Gershen Kaufman, Ph.D., and Lev Raphael, Ph.D., is a seventy-six page book packed with specific how-to's for home and classroom use. Children who can learn to defend and assert themselves can give up the victim role.

A child who is being put down can respond passively, assertively, or aggressively. Here are three examples to illustrate the difference:

<u>Put Down #1</u>: *"You're too fat to play with us."*

Passive Response (unspoken): *No one ever wants to be with me.*

Assertive Response (spoken): *"I've been working on my free throws. I think I could make some points for your team."*

Aggressive Response (spoken): *"Look who's talking. You run like a pig."*

<u>Put Down #2</u>: *"Here comes Betty. Look at those watermelons!"*

Passive Response (unspoken): *I hate my body.*

Assertive Response (spoken): *"That's out of line. I treat you with respect and I expect the same from you."*

Aggressive Response (spoken): *"It takes a fruit to know a fruit."*

<u>Put Down #3:</u> *"So how are you going to suck up with the teacher today, nerd?"*

Passive Response (unspoken): *I'm going to keep quiet in class. I won't raise my hand, even if I know the answer.*

Assertive Response (spoken): *"I'm proud of my grades. I'm going to need them to get into college."*

Aggressive Response (spoken): *"I'm just glad I'm not a retard, like you."*

For younger children, we recommend *A Children's Book About BEING BULLIED* by Joy Berry. It is part of a *Help Me Be Good* series and the illustrations make it very applicable. It is never too early to help children form assertive patterns.

Jacob was only three years old when he handled a situation like a pro. Jacob's grandmother took him to the library. In a play area set aside for younger children, Jacob spent about thirty minutes building a most elaborate construction with blocks that he carefully arranged. No sooner had he completed his engineering feat, when another child came up and casually destroyed his masterpiece. Jacob used his words. He said to the boy: "That was not a nice thing to do." But the boy just laughed and didn't seem ashamed so Jacob looked around the room until he found the boy's mother. He went up to her and told her that her son had done something that wasn't nice when he knocked over Jacob's block building. The mother heard Jacob's distress and responded by insisting that her son re-build Jacob's structure, at Jacob's instruction.

There are so many wonderful elements to that story. Jacob was very angry but he didn't seek revenge with physical force. He confronted his perpetrator but when there was no remorse he sought out an adult to intervene. An adult took a young boy's anguish seriously and taught her own son a lesson in restitution. These early, small steps can become the patterns of a lifetime.

Learning how to handle anger was a subject that came up in almost every discussion about bullying.

Two writers for the *Seattle Times*, Carol M. Ostrom and Lee Moriwaki, published an article "Anger is all the Rage" in the May 9, 1995, edition of the *St. Louis Post-Dispatch*. They interviewed a number of professionals to seek answers to questions such as: Are we angrier than we used to be? Does anger serve a purpose? What are the warning signs that anger is a problem? and How can we control anger so that it doesn't get out of hand?

Roland Maiuro, director of the anger management and do-mestic violence program at Harborview Medical Center in Seattle, thinks we are angrier than ever. "People experience that it is a meaner, more dangerous place than it used to be and they are arming themselves." Half the households in the United States now have firearms, Maiuro notes.

Anger, on the other hand, can serve a constructive purpose. It can warn us of danger and prepare us to take action to protect ourselves, it can motivate us to right a wrong or organize a group to tackle a problem. June Price Tangney, associate professor in clinical psychology at George Mason University in Virginia says that: "Most anger results not in violence or aggression, but in positive results, such as an improvement in behavior or a new understanding in a relationship."

If anger can be helpful or hurtful, how can we know when it has become a negative force? In the same *Seattle Times* article, seven warning signs were listed to determine whether or not a child has a problem with anger.

Warning Signs For Children

1. Seems constantly on edge, irritable, and angry. Attempts to resolve the problem provide no relief.
2. Becomes physically aggressive and can't seem to stop aggressive impulses. Acts before he or she thinks. Has difficulty learning from experience. Relies on hitting, grabbing.
3. Exhibits punitive or cruel behavior toward pets or animals.
4. Lacks social behavior, such as sharing or waiting one's turn. Has few friends or no lasting friends.
5. Misreads social cues. Interprets other children's behavior as hostile. Thinks, for instance, that because another youngster looks at him, the child has bad thoughts about him.
6. Blames others and does not take responsibility for his or her own role in a conflict.
7. Often argues with adults and defies or refuses to comply with adults' requests.

Helping Children Deal With Anger

1. Encourage children to express their anger in words. Even if they express disrespectful anger at you, separate the two expressions, such as: "It's okay for you to be upset and angry with me for not letting you do what you want, but it's not okay for you to talk to me that way."

2. Show them that you really listened by repeating what they said and expressing some understanding of their feelings.

3. Discuss their reason for being angry. Is it because they are disappointed, sad, frustrated, jealous? The more children can understand the source of their anger, the better equipped they will be to deal with it themselves.

4. Let them cool off. Put a younger child in Time Out until they can get control of their feelings. Advise an older child that they need to take time to collect their emotions.

5. Recommend exercise. Help children dissipate some of the anger energy by engaging in some physical activity.

6. Have them take some deep breaths. Offer suggestions that have calming effects—a warm bath, soothing music, etc.

7. Focus on finding a creative solution.

8. Distract them by involving them in something that requires their attention and energy.

9. Share a lesson about how you have learned to handle your anger.

10. Suggest that they draw a picture to describe their anger or write a letter, poem, or story.

For victims who want to consider the most promising response, each situation requires a thoughtful game plan. I recall a situation where Jason, a fine-looking, mature seventh-grade student was being pushed to fight back by his parents who were suffering with him. His sin was that he was at least two heads taller than most of the students in his class and for this he had earned the label of the Jolly Green Giant. The unremitting teasing was interfering with his school work. He could easily have used his height and weight to his advantage, but fighting was not in his nature and he was eager to find another alternative. During our discussion he opted to share his feelings. He talked about how discouraging it was to hear the same taunts over and over again. He explained that there was nothing he could do about being so tall. He spoke of dreading to come to school each day. And then he thanked two loyal friends who made his life bearable. They were the shortest boys in the class and obviously had come in for their own share of teasing. But they had used their height as a bond and formed a victim support group. Some children were affected by what they heard and chose not to continue the badgering. Jason fought back, with words instead of his fists.

Jameel handled it in a slightly different way. A bully singled out Jameel as his target and picked on him day after day. Jameel told his parents about the annoying boy who was physically and verbally taunting him. His father advised him to fight back, to "teach the bully a lesson" while his mother cautioned him against fighting and encouraged him to find another way to solve the problem. One day when he arrived home, the bully was waiting for him on the front stoop, prepared for battle. Jameel looked him in the eye and said: "My father wants me to punch you out and my mother wants me to try to work it out without fighting. I don't know what to do, so I'm going to let you decide." The bully was so taken aback by the offer he retreated and never bothered Jameel again.

Fighting is discouraged as a solution by all the experts who have researched bullying, yet it is always mentioned by students in every discussion.

In her book, *Deadly Consequences—How Violence Is Destroying Our Teenage Population and a Plan to Begin Solving the*

Problem, Deborah Prothrow-Stith, M.D., discusses a lesson in her violence prevention curriculum that engages the students in a cost/benefit analysis of fighting. One class created the following list:

What's Good And What's Bad About Fighting	
Good	**Bad**
winning	kill someone
prove your point	get killed
get a reputation	might lose
get attention	get embarrassed
enjoyment	get suspended from school
relieves tension	get expelled
evens the score	lose a job
satisfaction	get a bad reputation
earn money (become a pro)	no one wants to hang out with you because you're always fighting
	have an enemy coming after you
	revenge cycle begins
	get clothes dirty or torn
	get scarred for life
	may have to pay for broken things
	lose respect of friends
	parents responsible for medical bills
	get punished
	hurt innocent bystanders
	hurt a person (then be sorry)

Any attempts to persuade students not to fight will have to offer plausible alternatives. Ann Bishop, a teacher who works with Prothrow-Stith's violence prevention curriculum always tells her students that the best way to respond to insults is with a nondefensive question:

"Why would you want to say that?"

"Why would you want to tell me I am ugly (or dumb, or fat) and hurt my feelings?"

There is yet another option for those who don't wish to fight. A number of children have reported that they took karate lessons and were able to use martial arts techniques to defend themselves without attacking back. Karate proved to be a successful confidence builder, as well as an effective defense strategy. One adult that I interviewed spoke of his solution many years ago before karate was popular. He joined the boxing team at his school. He never had to throw a punch outside of a match, but the bullies who had pestered him kept their distance.

As for a "hug," Melvin Woods, a school counselor at a private middle school in Kansas City, admits that it is an unusual tactic but he is enthusiastic about its effectiveness. During a series of training sessions for peer-abuse intervention, he recommended hugging. The first response was a lot of snickering and squirming. But Melvin persisted with his theory that what a bully needs is what he lacks—affection, caring, warmth of relationship. Time after time, Melvin's entreaties were met with giggles but, one morning, one of the student trainees came into the session in a really foul mood. Some incident before school had really worked him up and he was hot with rage. Melvin approached him, put his arms around him and said: "What you need is a hug!"

At first the student was stunned, but then he grinned and relaxed into the arms of his hugger. The tension was eased and the class broke into applause. Melvin pursued the concept with his students as they discussed the possible benefits and repercussions. The students finally agreed that it might be possible to establish "the hug" as a preventive strategy, if nothing else. Some students might appreciate a hug but others might exert self control just to avoid the ominous squeeze. For the idea to work, most students felt that hugging would have to become a social norm for the school and used with humor. But it was acknowledged as a defusing technique.

What Can a Witness Do?

Answers to this question have evolved into a continuum of options, from those that demand the least risk to those that require the greatest courage.

The option of least jeopardy is to withhold support from the bully by not participating in a hurtful event. Under no circumstances, encourage a bully with laughter or words. Paula and I have often wondered about the long-lasting effect on those students who cheered the bullies who antagonized Zack, the student who shot his school principal.

A witness can choose not to repeat gossip or give credence to the gossiper. The "he said, she said" conversations are a major cause of pain and violence. Students, as well as adults, are not immune to the titillation of exposed secrets, even if they are untrue. There are any number of successful magazines that thrive on the public appetite for gossip. Restricting the spread of malicious rumors and dethroning the power of the gossipmonger is a very important role a neutral student can play. As one student so aptly put it: "Today, it's Debra, tomorrow it could be me!"

One high-school class was going to propose a survey with a subsequent editorial on the topic of gossip to the editor of the school newspaper in hopes of getting school-wide attention focused on the subject. Gossip is consistently mentioned as a source of great pain for many students, especially girls.

The handwritten note about Stephanie spread through the class like wildfire. By lunch, everyone had read it. Stephanie was an outstanding student. Her breasts had developed early and she was the envy of many girls, especially, Corinne. The note Corinne penned implied that the reason Stephanie made such good grades was because she had "made out" with the math teacher. Stephanie was mortified and didn't want to return to school. Instead, she empowered herself to learn the identity of the author of the hateful note and then reported the information to the principal. Corinne was questioned and suspended from school for three days. Once the issue was brought to the attention of school authorities, the swift, firm punishment by the administration served notice on malicious gossip and nothing similar has happened since. Stephanie chose to take action rather than be defeated by her bully but there were many opportunities for a witness to refuse to pass the note on and toss it away.

Another assignment for students is to consider the pressure they put on each other to conform and the prejudices that motivate their actions. "Fitting in" becomes a driving force for young people and tolerance for differences is not the norm. Fashion is considered an important test of peer loyalty. Students who cannot afford the clothing status symbols are raw bait for teasing. Starter jackets, caps, certain brands of athletic shoes, and jewelry are not only desirable, they can become a self-esteem requirement. The financial pressure some students feel is so great, they resort to stealing—or worse! A number of schools have adopted uniforms or some modified clothing code to relieve the wardrobe pressure on students and families. Many parents and teachers have given high marks to the school uniform solution. A recent *USA Today* article by Dennis Kelly reported on a survey of 5,500 secondary school principals, 70 percent think uniforms could cut down on violence. But gray pants and plaid skirts, however helpful they may be, are no substitute for prodding young people to be responsible for their behavior and more open-minded about differences of all kinds.

At the next level a student can support a victim in private. Without identifying themselves to the bully, they could let the victim know that they are concerned and offer kindness. Many a victim I have interviewed, spoke of the yearning for a comforting word. Simple recognition of their predicament would have been a blessing compared to the isolation so many victims undergo.

A witness can alert an adult that a bullying situation is occurring. We have spoken of the fact that many mother's complaints are discounted and chalked up to overprotectiveness. Documentation given by a neutral student could be important supporting evidence for a concerned parent.

A witness might be in a position to take a bully aside and appeal to his better nature, using humor or genuine praise to counter a lack of self-esteem. Once, I suggested to some students that someone might say something, like "I don't think you're a cruel person and you may not realize how much you're hurting Ray." Some of the kids started laughing so I asked them what was so funny. They informed me that real kids don't talk like that. I asked them to put it in their language and they said: "Cool it, man. Get off Ray's back!"

Moving up the continuum of courage, a witness could offer support to a victim in the presence of the bully. They could retrieve the victim's books or say something like "You don't deserve to be treated that way."

Juliet is only three-years-old but she has the empathy and courage of someone much older. At her preschool, a small vixen named Maxine had already learned how to terrorize her peers. One recent morning, Juliet was a bystander when Maxine went up to Robbie and informed him that his mother was never going to come back for him. No words could cause more panic for a three-year-old! Juliet went over to Robbie and assured him that his mommy would come and get him, just like she did every day. Robbie's tears and Maxine disappeared.

The most forceful tactic for a witness is to confront a bully. Most bullies are never challenged so they continue to prey on weaker students. A confident, skilled student might be willing to wrest power from a perpetrator but this is no task for someone whose own status is marginal.

One of the most inventive solutions in which a witness confronted a bully occurred on a bus. Keneisha was the target of abusive teasing. She was teased because she was overweight and because she was an African American. Jay had just moved to this new school from a smaller community where some adult would have said: "Stop that!" But the abuse continued and no one intervened. Jay came home and told his father about his dilemma. Jay felt his only choice was to fight one of the bullies and get beaten up himself. His father encouraged him to use his creativity to find another way—and he did! Jay had played the role of Ebenezer Scrooge in the school production of a Christmas Carol, so the next morning when the teasing routine aimed at Keneisha began, Jay stood up, gesturing grandly and declared in his most Dickensian voice: "I am acutely aware of the fact that there are some crabby people on this bus. Now, no one knows more about being crabby than Ebenzer Scrooge. I perfected the art and learned, to my dismay, that I was miserable and making everyone else miserable. So I say Bah to teasing and humbug to making fun of someone." His passenger/audience was stunned into silence and attacked Keneisha, nevermore.

Keneisha's situation brings up the topic of racism, which is a source of bullying in many schools that we've visited. Teachers and principals will tell us that it is a problem but it is difficult to get the children to openly discuss discrimination. Younger students are more willing to admit that they are called names because of their skin color, but by the time they reach middle school or high school the effects of racism have become more ingrained. As one teacher said: "The hopeful anger has been replaced by hopeless bitterness." Racism is another example of a situation that has been with us for so long we are like the frog who got cooked. We've gotten so accustomed to the simmering hostility, we've lost our ability to recognize the seething racism for what it is. Jay was remarkable for his courage and inventiveness, but we cannot expect each witness to singlehandedly challenge the injustices of our society.

When the challenges are beyond the scope of one brave crusader, several witnesses can join forces to protect a victim. There are many possibilities for a group of students to attempt to do something that might be hazardous for one student alone. For instance, they could walk someone home who dreads the vulnerability of walking alone. They could assert school standards and norms such as "Cruelty is unacceptable here," "We don't allow bullying in our school," "No one has the right to hurt someone else." They could devise clever ploys in specific situations.

Take the case of Derek, a small, wiry, hyperactive, extremely bright fourth-grader. In a small brainstorming group, he described in great detail the physical and verbal abuse he received from the larger boys in his class. The scariest time for him was recess, when the bullies plotted their most devious tricks. His self-protection plan consisted of anticipating when the class would be excused and making a dash to a hill that served as his hiding place until the liberating whistle was blown. This had been his pattern of behavior for two years. He longed to climb the junglegym, play kickball, or engage in other recess activities, but the risk was too great. In a brainstorming session with a group of students in Derek's school, someone came up with the solution for a group of students to form a "human moat" around him until the bullies got tired of trying to reach him. Whether the witnesses were brave enough to match their inventiveness with action, I do not know, but one creative, courageous plan that was enacted received national attention.

In Oceanside, California, Ian O'Gorman, a fifth-grade student shaved his head in anticipation of chemotherapy treatments for lymphoma. Thirteen of his buddies joined him at the barbershop, where they too, became bald. "The last thing he would want is to not fit in, to be made fun of, so we just wanted to make him feel better and not left out," said Kyle Hanslik who initiated the idea.

During a discussion about the role of witnesses with a group of fifth- and sixth-graders in the school gym, a young girl sitting in the upper stands of the bleachers timidly raised her hand and asked: "What if someone is picking on a girl, and she's not my friend. In fact, what if I don't like her, do I have to stick up for her?" The group became unusually silent. The discussion about bullying had become a forum on ethics. I had never been asked that question before and as usual, I looked to the wisdom of the group for the answer.

A boy in the front row said: "Yes."

"Why?" I asked.

And the reply came: "Because she's a human being."

If you had been there, I suspect you would have had tears in your eyes, too. In Plattsburg, Missouri, where young people are struggling with all the angst that comes with pre-adolescence, in a world that bombards them with more violent messages than ones of moral spirit, I was deeply moved by the honesty of the question and the beauty of the answer.

Conflict-mediation and conflict-resolution programs are spreading all across the country as school administrators seek to involve students in a structured format to reduce violence. Conflict resolution is a problem-solving process that can be taught in classrooms for use by everyone in their interpersonal relations. Any approach to conflict-resolution skill training would include an emphasis on listening, learning how to sort out and express feelings, brainstorming for optional ways to solve a problem, and coming to an agreement that both parties can accept—a win/win solution. Conflict mediation is a specific skill used by a trained mediator or team of mediators to assist two or more parties who are willing to work out an agreement. Mediators are trained to honor confidentiality, to listen without judgment, to establish a set of acceptable ground rules for constructive discussion, and to help the disputing parties find a compatible solution resulting in a signed, written contract. Even elementary school students can be trained to be effective mediators. Students who complete the peer-mediation training speak gratefully for the changes it has made in their own lives, much less the lives of the students they counsel. Teachers and students with whom I have spoken attest to the calmer atmosphere in the school environment when the mediation principles become institutionalized.

Community service is a marvelous strategy. It's a glorious win/win situation. The people who receive assistance benefit and the students who give of themselves benefit by acquiring self-confidence, social skills, compassion, and learning to take responsibility. The National Crime Prevention Council found that when schools mandated participation in community service, the dropout rate declined. A creative way to combine community service and the prevention of bullying is a successful program that is based on the concept of "learning by teaching." Following a presentation on the topic of bullying to a middle school in Kansas City, Missouri, students were recruited to work in teams of three or four with classrooms of third- and fourth-grade youngsters to promote kindness. Forty-two students volunteered to attend a series of eight training sessions that began an hour before regularly scheduled classes. Over 80 percent of the volunteer students stayed with the project through completion.

Their training covered information about bullies and victims; empathy exercises; role playing scenarios; peer issues; physical, verbal, and emotional abuse; trust building; and creative problem solving.

For logistical reasons, the middle-school volunteers had only one opportunity to work with the younger students. Both the student teachers and student pupils looked forward to their kindness session that was held at the end of the semester. When the presentation day arrived, the "teachers" were excited and nervous. Each team of student teachers focused on one of the themes from their training and engaged the third- and fourth-graders in lively interaction for an hour. Some of the teams were clearly more effective than others, but all of them accomplished the task. When it was over, the student instructors wished that they could have had at least one more chance to work with the children. It would be hard to assess the impact of the subject matter on the younger students. The greatest benefit was clearly on the ledger of the middle-school student-teachers who gained so much in the preparation for their teaching assignment. The intent, all along, was to capture the interest of the hard-to-reach seventh and eighth grade population in the subject matter of bullying and this was accomplished.

In summary, power is a major factor in bullying. Bullies acquire destructive power at the expense of children who feel powerless. Children who obtain more power than they can handle, or who use power to abuse and exploit are in peril of forming behavior patterns that will follow them throughout the course of their life. They may become wife batterers or child abusers, abusive employers, difficult neighbors—people who thrive on troublemaking. Bullies who maintain control over their peers can prevent their victims from learning how to make healthy life choices. Bullies who are allowed to terrorize students and teachers create an atmosphere of fear and insecurity that undermines learning and influences some of our best teachers to pursue other careers. Bullies who use power to create havoc for their siblings or step-brothers/sisters destroy the trust and safety that children need to count on from their family. Consequently, there are many situations that will require adults to step in and take control. In the next chapter we will spell out strategies for parents, teachers, and school administrators, but fundamentally adults can intervene by empowering young people to deal with bullying themselves. This can be done by conducting discussions about bullying that present a clear understanding of the choices and consequences in store for bullies, victims, and witnesses. Sometimes students may shift from one role to the other, i.e., bullies become victims, victims become bullies, and a bystander may quickly find him or herself in a victim situation as a result of moving to a new school, an accident, an illness, a betrayed friendship, a weight gain, or a combination of factors. These discussions can take place in schools but they can also take place in religious groups, day-care programs, scout troops, sports activities, recreation centers, and, of course, home.

Discussions that deflate bullies and give them insight into their antisocial behavior can be very effective but discussions without follow-through are not enough. Children need information, they need skills, and they need support to meet the challenge. Our task is to provide them with the information, skills, and support and then give them opportunities to be successful.

Bullies can be monitored, punished, and converted. Victims can be acknowledged, supported, and empowered. And witnesses can play the most pivotal role of all in maneuvering power issues. Young people thrive on being needed. Celebrating their accomplishments can be our greatest gift.

For example, a television station or a local newspaper could be persuaded to do a feature story about the classes that are making a difference or the P.T.A. could host a pizza party when everyone has gone a whole month without anyone being teased. While incentives are a means to an end, the ultimate lesson to be learned is that virtue is its own reward and kindness brings pleasure to both the giver and the receiver.

Young people know better than the rest of us how high the cost of bullying is. They need to understand that it is within their power to reduce the toll.

CHAPTER TEN

Strategies for Adult Intervention

"My child is going through hell and it's killing me"

MANY PARENTS WORRY about their children's future, wondering how their children will navigate through the overwhelming problems that characterize our time. Drug abuse, sexually transmitted diseases, challenging economic conditions, and the violence that seems to permeate every aspect of contemporary life present staggering problems without ready solutions. Bullying, however, is an issue that can be remedied. This chapter will focus on the role that parents, teachers, and child advocates can play.

"My son is going through hell. What can I do to help him?"

"Our principal is extremely concerned about a bullying situation. We feel like we're sitting on a time bomb. There must be something we can do."

"My daughter can't take any more of this. We're going to have to transfer her to another school or move."

"My son is a bully and when I ask him how it makes him feel when he hurts somebody, he says he doesn't care."

These are some of the comments we heard when we met with parents and teachers over the past several years.

There are six types of interactions in which adults can make a difference.

1. Parents with their own children.
2. Parents with other children.
3. Parents with other parents.
4. Parents with teachers and school administrators.
5. Teachers with students.
6. Adults as community advocates.

PARENTS WITH THEIR OWN CHILDREN

The home plays a pivotal role because children have formed strong patterns of social interaction by the time they enter school. Core values that can prevent bullying from ever occurring need to be taught from the beginning. By the age of five, children will know if cruelty is unacceptable in their family or not. For children with siblings, there will be countless opportunities for parents or guardians to supervise their children as normal competitive situations occur. Fights with brothers and sisters in which cruelty erupts give excellent "teachable moments" when adults can assert their principles.

Teaching children to handle pets and animals will give parents another opportunity to communicate values about compassion and empathy. Abuse of animals is often the first indication that a child's anger or aggression is out of proportion.

Your most important task is to love your child with all your heart and soul. Uri Bronfenbrenner, a noted authority in the field of child development, is known for urging parents to be absolutely crazy about their children. Cherish every quality of your child's being and let them know it day after day after day.

If you, the parent, did not receive the unconditional love that children thrive on, be aware of the imprint that those early experiences may have left on you. Do all that you can to resolve any anger, hurts, bitterness, or behavior patterns that you may be handing down to your offspring. There are many books that can help you explore past memories in a wholesome way. There are Parenting Education classes and support groups in many communities.

Parents As Teachers (PAT) is a wonderful program for families with children from birth to three years of age that is available through many school systems. PAT provides a trained parent-educator, free of charge, to come to the home to be a personal resource to the family on any topic relating to parenting and respond to parents' questions and concerns. The parent–educator will stay in contact with your family during those apprehensive preschool years. Some programs continue to kindergarten entry.

Mental health centers and religious institutions frequently offer parenting programs. Parents Anonymous has been providing support services for almost thirty years to individuals and families who recognize they have problems coping with the tasks of parenting. There are parent nurturing groups that help people work through some of the physical and emotional deficits from their childhood. Counselors and therapists are trained to help adults break the cycle of abuse that is passed on from generation to generation.

The indispensable gift of self-esteem may be the most important legacy we can leave to our children as they face a world beyond our protection. When we are consumed by our own self-doubts, it is more difficult to persuade our children of their worth. Building self-esteem in a child is a primary factor in the prevention of bullying behavior—for bullies as well as victims.

Even if you have given your child unrationed amounts of love and praise, it is entirely possible that he or she will be picked on by others. It might be because your child is unusually bright or talented. Your son or daughter might be short or tall, heavy or thin, or have any one of a number of physical characteristics that will single him or her out for teasing. Don't ever take a child's

positive self-image for granted. Affirm your children at every opportunity and assure him or her that he or she has not caused the
distress. The problem lies with the bully, but your child must
learn how to cope with it.

One child psychiatrist found that parents were amazed at
how quickly the problem could be solved when the victim/child
became convinced that he or she was not at fault and it was the
bully who was the source of the predicament. Giving up the self-
blame that accompanies bullying may be all it takes for a victim
to interrupt the pattern. When children who have failed to stand
up for themselves can be convinced to take control, the problem
can be solved most directly. Discuss a range of options and talk
with your child about each one in detail. What may work with
one bully may not work with another. A would-be teaser may be
discouraged when his or her taunting is ignored. If the bully
wants attention or a reaction and it isn't forthcoming, the game
may be over. Even when your child has ignored the bully's jibes,
however, it doesn't mean that the words haven't stung. Offer to
be an outlet for the hurt and anger that is felt but not expressed
at the perpetrator.

When ignoring the bully doesn't work, assertive training
just might. One parent told us of such "training" that her child
received in preschool, at the age of three. Stephan was a serious
child. He would rather work a puzzle or play with building
blocks than roughhouse with toy weapons. Mario, on the other
hand, was always on the go—running at full speed, charging
anyone in sight. Stephan was almost always Mario's chosen
target. If he wasn't chasing Stephan, he was teasing him and
knocking his blocks over. Stephan's parents had always discouraged him from fighting. Fortunately, they selected a day care
center that promoted nonviolence and taught the children to
"use your words." Every parent could teach his or her child this
technique. The training teaches language responses that begin
with "I" messages, such as: "I wish you would leave me alone."
"Please don't tease me. I don't like it when you knock my

buildings over." Stephan rehearsed the phrases with his parents and the next time he was approached by Mario, he spoke them firmly. It took several repetitions before the teasing stopped, but the success stayed with the youngster and the mother claims that her son, who is now ten-years-old, continues to use this tactic in many facets of his life.

Some parents believe that the only way a bully can be stopped is for the victim to "punch his lights out." Parents who advise their children to duke it out risk encouraging a confrontation that may result in serious injury. Many children become victimized because they do not defend themselves, but we believe that there are many options that do not require violence. Violence most often begets more violence and each retaliation escalates dangerously. There are too many tragic cases that are testimony to the consequences of physical force.

Teaching children to manage their anger is a critical task of parenting. Families in particular and society in general need to find a better way to deal with the anger and rage that is so prevalent. Within the twentieth century we have seen the pendulum swing from a time of repressed anger that caused serious forms of depression and other psychiatric illnesses to an era of unrestrained anger that is dangerous for everyone. It is time for the pendulum to swing to the center and this task must fall to parents, through lesson and example. Being a role model is the most persuasive lecture you will ever give.

Children will invariably suggest humor as a strategy to defuse a bully. Be sure to include it as part of the repertoire of responses. One boy was reported to have joked a determined abuser into being his friend. He kept making him laugh until he gave up and decided instead to enjoy his company. Whenever you can enable your child to triumph over a testy situation by his own wit, you have planted a fertile seed of confidence.

Storytelling is an excellent tool. Children love to hear about stories that actually happened when you were their age. Share a real event that occurred when you were young. Maybe you handled a bully in a successful way or you observed someone else's mastery. Describe a victim situation in your school and talk about the reaction you had at the time. An established businessman, who was the butt of countless jokes in his youth because of his height, has resolved his childhood pain by instilling in his children a deep concern for the feelings of others. He promised himself that he would stress the value of compassion when he became a father and is quite proud that his sons are so caring toward others.

Have discussions with your children about the various types of bullying. Help them understand the differences between physical, verbal, emotional, and sexual abuse. It is important for children to understand the complex array of behaviors that constitute bullying. Students can usually give accurate examples of physical, verbal, and sexual abuse but have some difficulty defining emotional abuse. Rejecting, ignoring, isolating, terrorizing, and corrupting—the five forms of emotional abuse delineated by James Garbarino, Ph.D.—are not easily identified by children. These behaviors are more subtle, and perhaps more difficult to target but they are equally damaging. When children come to understand that these actions are a part of bullying, young people might be kinder or at least eliminate some unintentional abuse.

Another benefit that can be derived from this discussion is to help some children realize that there is a valid basis for the vague feelings of discomfort they have when they are around an emotionally bullying child. Precisely because these behaviors are not always obvious, it can be extremely valuable for young people to have an expanded vocabulary to express their hurt, angry, or sad feelings.

Teach your children about empathy. Do some role playing with them about a conflict they are having with someone else. After they have strongly defended their position, call for a role reversal. Now it is your turn to play *their* part, and have them play the part of the other party. You can't begin empathy training too early. Empathetic feelings can be developed for a baby brother or sister, a pet, an aging grandparent. The possibilities are endless. At one parent session on this topic, a mother reported that her child used empathy as a successful technique to deflate a bully. When the bully verbally attacked her child, her response was to counter with words like "You know, some days I just get into the foulest mood and I start picking on other people even when they haven't done anything to me. Are you having a bad day?"

In his book *The Human Mind* Dr. Karl Menninger tells the tale of a lonely fish in a well-populated fish pond. "When a trout, rising to a fly gets hooked on a line and finds himself unable to swim about freely, he begins a fight which results in struggles and splashes and sometimes an escape. Often, of course, the situation is too tough for him. In the same way the human being struggles with his environment and with the hooks that catch him. Sometimes he masters his difficulties; sometimes they are too much for him. His struggles are all that the world sees and it usually misunderstands them. It is hard for a free fish to understand what is happening to a hooked one." Dr. Karl then relates the fable to the possible times we humans reject others whose behavior offends us without realizing that they may have a metaphorical hook in their mouth and are doing the best they can under the circumstances.

In every school, in every part of the country, children report being teased because they are "different." Glasses, braces, height, weight, and clothing are the first factors mentioned by students, but skin color is rarely stated, even when racism is a considerable source of peer tension. Racial undercurrents in school are no different than the racial issues in society at large. They are masked and unspoken, but present, nevertheless. If our heterogeneous society is to flourish we must learn to be comfortable with our individual differences. Consider this story told by a thirteen-year-old seventh-grade client of Paula's. Liz has mild cerebral palsy due to complications at birth and was then successfully treated for cancer as a young child. As a result of her illnesses, Liz is small in stature and has a slight limp. Liz is also a talented artist and in the academically gifted program. One boy at school teased her frequently, which hurt her feelings deeply. Liz and Paula discussed the situation, the foolishness of our culture's obsession with appearances and looking a certain way. Liz made a sensitive observation that came from her experience as a bird breeder. She had learned that birds are resistant to mating with birds who have different markings than themselves and wondered if the intolerance of human beings isn't perhaps a "natural" response. Paula countered that many animals "naturally" engage in behavior that humans find unacceptable. We expect more of ourselves and if accepting differences doesn't come naturally, we know we can teach ourselves to behave appropriately. If we are not ready to "love our neighbors as ourselves" we can still treat them with the respect that our system of justice demands.

Some children are so fearful of being "different," they will not speak up in class or try to make good grades. The consequences of withholding knowledge can be devastating and parents have a quintessential role to play in emphasizing the value of respect for others as early as possible. Initiate conversations with your children that stress the importance of making wise choices and doing the right thing in the face of peer pressure. Help them to move from accepting differences with others to self acceptance. It is simply impossible to please others all the time.

Rene Russo, a successful model and actress, who has appeared on the covers of *Vogue* and *Glamour* magazines, gave an interview in the December 3, 1995, issue of *Parade* magazine. She described her early years, which included wearing a body cast for four years. "I looked liked a bear," she said, "and I felt very unattractive. Kids are cruel, and a lot of them made fun of me. I remember walking down the hall and someone calling me 'Jolly Green Giant.' At that age, you want to feel that you fit in, and I was like an oddity. I think that's a lot of reason for my low self-esteem."

She dropped out of school in the tenth grade. "I just couldn't handle how hateful they were to me. Maybe if I'd had more self-confidence, they wouldn't have bothered me, but I didn't. I became a real loner. I spent a lot of time in my room with the door shut." For Rene, the self-esteem didn't come until many years later. It wasn't the money, the attention, the starring roles in movies. For Rene it was studying theology and having faith that gave her the personal strength to accept herself.

Children will face many temptations along the way and children who have been inculcated with a strong sense of right and wrong will fare better than peers who surrender their best interest to the whim of the group. Talk to your child about the immorality of silence when cruelty has taken over.

PARENTS WITH OTHER CHILDREN

If your child has tried a number of tactics and none of them have caused the bully to back down or give up, consider talking to the bully yourself. It is best to get your child's permission to pursue this move. If such permission is denied, you have to weigh the options of remaining silent or intervening. One mother told of a boy who continued to knock her son off of his bicycle. Her son's entreaties were to no avail. On a daily basis he was attacked on the way home from school. One day the mother approached the bully and announced she would not tolerate such behavior. She informed him that there were laws against assault and battery and if he did not desist, she would discuss the matter with his parents. If necessary, she would take the matter to court. Her successful formula consisted of being respectful; remaining calm, but firm; presenting the facts; and stating a plan of action. The bullying stopped.

Some parents report that they have arranged a meeting with the bully and their child. The purpose is to allow each student to tell his/her story about the situation and serve in a mediating capacity. One parent told of calling the bully on the telephone and inviting him to their home. She said that she had learned that there are always two sides to every story and she was eager to hear his version of the conflict. Though it is difficult to be objective when your child's stress and anxiety are carried around with you daily like a stone in your heart, the process of bringing two young people together to discuss a situation can sometimes be all that is required to alleviate the problem. Dealing with a bullying situation in such a straightforward, problem solving manner is preferable to avoidance or physical confrontation. It's important to demonstrate courage, firmness, and listening skills to your children. These strengths can be used more effectively than physical force.

Car pools, Brownie and Cub Scout meetings, slumber parties, and the like, can be wonderful opportunities to tackle the subject of bullying in general. If you feel tentative about bringing it up, rehearse several lead-ins until you find one that is the most comfortable for you to pursue. I find that asking children for their opinions rather than lecturing them is very productive. Sometimes situations can be nipped in the bud before they get out of hand. The tendency, however, is to hope that the matter will take care of itself and not "make an issue." Once you are convinced that bullying is not a benign rite of passage but a serious problem, you will be more inclined to act with courage to stop it.

PARENTS WITH OTHER PARENTS

Contacting a bully's parent or parents can be a risky strategy. Several authorities strongly oppose this approach and advise parents to take the matter to a teacher or principal. If the parent is someone you know, you might want to handle the situation personally rather than have them contacted by a third party.

Even so, you should anticipate a range of possible responses. One might be the parent who is shocked to hear that there is a problem and expresses appreciation for the contact. Another might be a parent who denies any possibility that his or her child is guilty of abusive behavior. There is the risk that the parent will become very angry and say hurtful things about your child. How you handle the communication process will be as important as the outcome, especially if your child is aware of your approach. If you envision yourself as a problem solver rather than an adversarial champion, your words as well as your tone of voice will follow your premise. The tone of your voice, especially on the phone when other facial cues are not accessible, can be very revealing. While you may be concentrating on your words, the listener will pick up on your "music."

If you are reluctant to confront another parent, consider the possibility of organizing a parents' meeting and inviting an expert to speak on the subject. Chances are you will find that you are not the only parent who is dealing with this problem. I have sat in on countless parent sessions, P.T.A. meetings, and have always been impressed with the wisdom that surfaces in such discussions. Some parents are quite willing to express their anguish and there is always a supportive response from others present. On one occasion, a father announced to the group that his daughter was "going through hell" and it was killing him. She would tell her parents about the gossip and the rumors that were being spread, but she would NOT disclose the name of the offender. In despair, the father plead with the other parents for advice. The compassion for this dad was overwhelming. People in the room tried in every way to ease his pain—through comments, questions, sharing. One mother implored the group to keep in mind that it was important to have compassion for the parents of the bully as well. She acknowledged that several years prior, her older son had been identified as the student who was making someone's life miserable on the bus. She and her husband were horrified and she observed that parents don't wish to raise children who are bullies any more than they want to raise children who are victims.

Parents with Teachers and School Administrators

If you have tried to deal with the bullying problem directly but the situation continues to fester, another tactic is to involve the teacher. Teachers are often not aware of bullying that is happening outside of their classroom. Children who bully are usually careful to victimize their peers out of sight of adults who may intervene. Nevertheless, you might opt to approach the teacher to contact the parent of the bully. A teacher can be someone who has established a relationship with the other parent and can handle the subject in a tactful way.

The teacher and parent can develop a joint plan and continue to share information. The teacher can alert other school personnel such as playground supervisors, cafeteria monitors, physical education teachers, and bus drivers who can become sensitized to the special problem. By keeping a more watchful eye, a number of adults can take steps to confront the bully and spare the victim from having to take the step of "snitching."

Parents and teachers must curtail the power of bullies. Peer power issues are complicated and sometimes delicate because parents are eager for their children to be popular. Students tell us that many bullies gather a certain amount of popularity because of the power they accrue and parents of bullies are not inclined to interfere when their children's currency is at stake. Nevertheless, power is just as corrupting for children as it is for adults and children cannot be expected to develop their own code of fairness. A fascinating book, *Lord of the Flies,* by William Golding is recommended reading for anyone who doubts the potential malevolence of children when they are left to their own devices. Adults must take responsibility to set limits for children who overstep reasonable boundaries and empower neutral students and victims to operate from strength.

Bev Clevenger, Director of Applied Research, at the Learning Exchange, a not-for-profit independent Educational Resource Center in Kansas City, Missouri, believes that it is important to curtail bullying behavior as it first occurs. "When a bully abuses power it's hard for one person to be the determining factor in deflating a bully, be it teacher or peer. When the community makes it clear, however, that bullying is not tolerated and that message is given by enough people to convince the bully that his/her actions are unacceptable, bullying can be stopped. It's like a spark in the wastebasket—if everyone stands by and watches the flame it will soon get out of control and become a fire. Someone, everyone in the community has to respond immediately and decisively."

There are occasions where an appointment with the Principal or Vice-Principal is advised. The bully might be a student in a different classroom, the bullying incidents may be occurring on the way to or from school, the teacher may be unwilling to intervene or have handled a situation poorly. A principal who makes bullying prevention a high priority and responds to reports from teachers, parents, and students with sensitivity and respect is a blessing to the community. A parent can be very helpful to the principal by documenting the incidents that have occurred and the action taken to resolve matters prior to contacting the administrator. The duration and intensity of bullying events is important to record. Keep track of any conversations you have with your child, the bully, the bully's parents, and/or the teacher. Make notes about the questions or comments you make and the responses. It is very important to be accurate and to confirm what you hear from the other person, adult, or child. When feelings are running high, sometimes it is difficult to absorb someone's response objectively. Take the time to repeat what you hear and ask if you have heard the reply correctly. Explain that you want to be as clear and accurate as possible and that you are taking notes, rather than trusting your memory.

If the principal is uncooperative, a parent should be prepared to proceed to the superintendent and school board level, if necessary. Document, document, document throughout the entire process.

Parents can be more effective advocates for their child if they approach an administrator with an expectant attitude—expectant in the sense of approaching the administrator as an ally who will share your concern, rather than as an adversary who will be put on the defensive. A parent can request that the principal bring all of the parents and students linked in a bullying situation together.

A principal and a school counselor can create a neutral atmosphere to deal with tense feelings that might erupt.

Not all schools have counselors, but we have found them to be remarkable resources when they are part of the team. Many teachers will turn to a school counselor at the first sign of a bullying situation and find a creative ray of hope. We heard of one counselor who devised a plan with teachers to handle elementary school children who start to "lose it" in the afternoon.

There are certain students who find classroom confinement beyond their capacity to endure. They cannot keep their feelings and their hands to themselves. The plan consists of a clipboard and a "note." When the teacher feels the need to divert a student's attention, he/she will ask the unmanageable student to take a "note," along with the clipboard to the counselor. The counselor recognizes the clipboard as the instrument of diversion and will find some reason to talk with the student for a while and send him or her on to another school official for some supposed task. The clipboard is recognized by everyone as the teacher's need to relieve the particular student and the classroom from stress buildup and everyone cooperates to send the student on a fifteen or twenty minute journey that distracts the student and prevents a volatile situation from exploding.

There is one action step that gets our most enthusiastic endorsement—the appointment of a committee to develop a schoolwide policy on peer abuse prevention. A parent, a teacher, or administrator can request the creation of a school policy on bullying that will be understood and enforced by all. The ideal way to develop such a policy is for the principal to appoint representatives from the school (counselors, teachers, nurses, administrators), the student body, parents, and include a bus driver. Such a policy, once adopted, can be discussed in every classroom and every member of the school community can sign the document, acknowledging their awareness of the policies and the consequences for not adhering to them. Bullies, victims and witnesses should be included on any task force. Involving bullies may be a particularly effective strategy. The bully might come to see his/her behavior from a different perspective, or may be willing to make changes as he/she develops ownership in the policy making process. A committee can be a wonderful opportunity to forge a partnership between adults and young people that can carry over into concerns beyond bullying. Be sure to include a section on sexual harassment. The Minnesota School Boards Association has developed a Sample School Board Policy Prohibiting Harassment and Violence. It is a good model to use for consideration and we are reprinting it as Attachment B. Even though this model exists, it is very important to have the committee work together to define their own standards and feel a sense of ownership of the final product. A policy that doesn't breathe with the life force of its advocates will not endure.

Many schools are introducing conflict resolution and peer mediation programs at the elementary, middle, and senior high school levels.

An alternative that must be considered is transferring your child to another school, enrolling him or her in a private or parochial school, or even moving. While this seems to be a most drastic decision, for some families it has been the only solution that worked.

TEACHER WITH STUDENTS

A teacher can establish the classroom as a safety zone where bullying is not permitted and all must adhere to the rule on a consistent basis. A teacher can announce that bullying is dangerous, and he or she needs to be aware when personal safety is threatened. A conversation about the difference between snitching, tattling, and reporting is important.

Teachers can advise students on physical, verbal, emotional, and sexual bullying. Discussions in the classroom or the homeroom period can take care of some of the most blatant offenses.

Teachers can empower witnesses to take leadership roles in securing safety for all students, but still not abdicate their responsibility to protect victims.

In addition to these general suggestions, we had some wonderful interviews with teachers who shared some techniques they use to defuse bullying in their classrooms. One of them, a fourth-grade teacher takes a proactive, preventive approach to the bullying problem. At the beginning of each class year, she talks a lot with her students and stresses two issues:

"Everyone has a value" and "How do you fit in?" To underscore these ideas, she has created a large puzzle of all different shapes, sizes, and colors. Each puzzle piece is 4" by 5". Each student is given a piece of the puzzle and asked to put a picture of themselves in the center. When all the student pieces are put together, there are still many extra pieces that represent parents, the principal, cafeteria workers, and new students who might enter the class during the year.

The puzzle is used as a symbol to open discussion about people—no two are alike, but it is possible for all of the separate individuals to come together in a whole that makes sense and is very satisfying.

Another prevention activity she uses is to bring a wrapped package for every student. Each package is completely different. Some are quite large, others small. She uses bows, stickers, yarn, and a variety of wrapping papers to make each one unique. Each student is then invited to select a package and discuss why they chose a particular package and what they discovered inside.

Again, the packages are used as symbols to talk about what attracts us to certain appearances. The symbolism continues with conversation about the contents of the packages. The teacher emphasizes that each student is "so beautiful inside." She believes that learning how to get along is *most important* so she spends a great deal of time talking with her children about these issues— not only to prevent problems from occurring, but to deal with them when they do erupt.

When girls are having "friendship problems," she will invite them to stay in the classroom for lunch and spread a blanket on the floor, using an informal, picnic atmosphere to talk things out and help the students come to a creative solution that is agreeable to everyone.

She also has developed some special techniques to deal with a student who is a bully. She sets the tone for class involvement by sharing a "secret" about bullies. "They need our help." She encourages students to see the bully as a person to be nurtured rather than feared. She empowers the class to "take care of" the bully and casts the bully in the role of patient.

When a classroom bully has developed a pattern to seek negative attention and has not learned to get positive attention, she helps the class and the bully work together to affirm any positive behavior exhibited.

Whenever possible, she involves the bully in all class discussions about the disruptive actions that are causing conflict. If absolutely necessary, she will ask the bully to leave the room until he can take responsibility for his actions and the class can discuss what their responsibilities are, as well.

When all other methods to help the bully achieve self control have failed, she makes a pact with the troubled student. If he feels too angry or is too upset to handle his feelings, they develop a signal, such as a pencil placed on his desk in a certain way to flag her attention that he needs help at that moment.

On the playground, a bully who starts fights and intrudes on other children's games, is given clear boundaries on the blacktop surface in which he can move.

As the student becomes more responsible, he earns more space and can expand from one square, to half the surface, to the entire playground. If he abuses the space, he loses the privilege.

When a teacher is aware that a bully has targeted a victim in the classroom, there are a number of steps to pursue. For instance, a teacher can rearrange the seating chart. Separating a bully and a victim can reduce friction. One teacher told of a plot that worked successfully when she assigned a bully and a victim to the same small problem solving group. Once they became members of the same "team," the relationship changed. A teacher can reduce the stress of the "last chosen" by avoiding such set-ups. There are many ways to divide groups within the classroom without placing some children in jeopardy of not being selected time after time. Recently, a female physical education teacher observed that this is a particular problem in gym classes and the non-athletic students learn to dread the "choosing time." She further observed that most male physical education instructors were athletes when they were young and never experienced the ostracization that non-athletes endure. Therefore, they are less likely to consider alternatives to the team selection process that leaves some students in perpetual discomfort.

Youth sports, like recess, is fraught with opportunities for bullying. Children who join teams because they want to learn a skill and have fun can discover that the competition, the emphasis on winning, and the pressure is not the enjoyment they expected. Coaches who set good examples of sportsmanship, who believe in equity of playing time, and make sure that bullying behavior is not tolerated are unsung heroes.

If the child is being teased because of a "teacher's pet" label, the teacher can back off of public praising. If the child is vulnerable because of poor work and low self-esteem, the teacher can offer an extra boost of encouragement and/or assign a stronger student to be a "buddy." The "buddy" concept can be particularly helpful when a new student enrolls. Stories of initiation rites or isolation for students who have transferred from other schools are rampant.

There are a number of programs, curricula, and videos about bullying and violence prevention in circulation that can be introduced.

Teachers can consult with guidance counselors and administrators and request an in-service training session on the topic of bullying. A teacher can volunteer to serve on a committee to develop and maintain school policies on the subject.

Most of all teachers can realize that intervention of some kind is required and take responsibility for both preventive and responsive initiatives.

ADULTS AS COMMUNITY ADVOCATES

There is much that can be done beyond the home and the school. Mothers Against Drunk Driving clearly altered the social norm with their persuasive campaign against drinking and driving. Advocacy can be a very creative effort with exciting results.

Roger Von Oech, author of *A Whack on the Side of the Head*, says an advocate needs to combine the characteristics of an explorer, an artist, a judge, and a warrior.

As an explorer, an advocate must be able to move into unknown areas, pay attention to unusual patterns, and seek out a variety of information. Their first task is always to collect the data and do research to be able to state their case effectively.

As artist, an advocate must develop the ability to be open to new ideas, imagine what will be instead of what is, and not be afraid to challenge the status quo. Just as it takes courage for students to become assertive, adults who advocate must be willing to make waves and look for creative solutions.

As judge, an advocate must be willing to ask tough questions, of self and others. Finding the balance between reason and passion can be a Solomon-like task.

As warrior, an advocate must be committed to persevere in spite of obstacles, set-backs, and defeat. This problem will not be eliminated easily and requires the stamina of a marathon runner. Be assured that what is happening to your child, in your school, is happening all across this country. This issue needs pioneers who will put their shoulders to the wheel to push for universal support to address the issue of bullying. Once you have been drawn into this problem, for whatever reason, be the most effective spokesperson you can be. You might prevent pain for a grandchild who hasn't even been born.

Change is scary and many people will resist, but consider other changes that people have made for health reasons within the last two decades. People have been willing to give up smoking, salt, caffeine, red meat, fat, and alcohol, proving that even addictive patterns *can* be changed. The increasing level of violence in our society is clearly a menace to public health. Violent behavior must be added to the list of social toxins.

What successful steps can we use?

1. Collect data. In addition to any personal experiences that you have documented, clip articles from newspapers and magazines. Make a special effort to listen to any radio or television programs that deal with the issue and read magazine articles on the topic.
2. Identify individuals who will join you in the research. Ask a professional to design a brief survey instrument for you or use the one that is at the back of this book, Attachment A. Interview young people and adults about their experiences.
3. Engage groups such as the P.T.A.; Child Abuse Prevention organizations; Boy Scout and Girl Scout Councils; Campfire, Inc.; and guidance counselors; and teacher's associations. Ask them to inquire about information or materials that have surfaced in their fields.
4. Organize a resource bank of people and materials that can illuminate the problem and offer solutions. Whenever possible, involve young people in significant roles. Persuade your local library to become a Resource Center for videotapes, books, pamphlets, curriculum, and other reference materials.

5. Identify national and local experts who can speak on the topic in a compelling way and invite them to speak at P.T.A. meetings and community forums. You might even become the resident expert.

6. Involve the media. Arrange for radio, television, and newsprint interviews with experts.

7. Write a letter to the editor or a column about the issue in your local newspaper. Tie it in with a current event about child cruelty that has captured public interest.

8. Bring up the subject at social gatherings. Ask people if they think bullying is a problem, now or when they were in school. Spread the word through conversational networks to build support and momentum.

9. Get appointed to a Committee on Bullying Policies for your school. Offer to chair it, and work closely with the school system. Be sure to involve students!

10. Review existing laws. Determine if provisions for reporting and/or prosecuting child abuse acts include peer to peer terminology. Accountability for perpetrators is a key strategy in reducing bullying.

11. Subscribe to catalogues and collect information about workbooks, videotapes, books, and other materials that are in current use.

12. Capture the interest of people who can be important to the cause by bringing them together to critique and evaluate available materials that could be used in your school and community.

13. Ask local drama groups to develop sketches or plays that can be presented. Role playing can be an exciting vehicle to involve students in creating impromptu strategies.

14. Recognize, celebrate, acknowledge individuals and groups who are making a difference. Create a variety of ways to give positive feedback to people who make a commitment and follow through, including young people.

15. Don't forget the power of lawsuits. Sometimes court adjudication is the last but most effective resort. A number of parents have sought damages, not because they believe that any amount of money can compensate for their children's distress, but because they want to set a precedent to bring about change.

16. Become involved in larger issues that impact on bullying such as media violence, racism, and the accessibility of guns to young people.

17. Document your successes and your failures. Write articles for publication that will encourage others to replicate your process in other communities.

These are but a few suggestions. Once you get involved in the process of becoming a change agent, you will come up with many ideas of your own and tap into others' as well. Here is a cause that eagerly awaits a concerned cadre of people—people who dream of a kinder world where adults and young people join hands to become peacemakers in our hearths and hallways.

CHAPTER ELEVEN

Solutions and Successful Models

"Resources are abundant, but useless unless we use them."

IN THIS CHAPTER we are going to recap the suggestions that we've made throughout the book and look at some ideas, including model bullying prevention programs, that can be integrated into the home and classroom. Prevention is the cardinal principle here. We have suggested a range of responses and interventions, but the strategy that holds the most promise is the one that keeps the problem from arising in the first place.

To begin with, we must take the issue of bullying seriously and engage parents, teachers, school administrators, students, and youth workers in a series of steps.

The first step is to build a national consensus that bullying behavior is unacceptable and will not be tolerated in homes, schools, playgrounds, buses, or anywhere that children congregate.

Committees involving parents, students, and school personnel should be appointed to develop policies that focus on the wellbeing and safety of children. A standard code that details unacceptable behavior should be adopted, implemented and maintained in every school. Bullies, victims, and witnesses should be included on any committee. A partnership between adults and young people should be cultivated. Students will sense if they are being used for token participation and the real benefits of such a committee will be lost.

It is painful, but essential to admit—*children are abusing children* and child abuse committed by children should be treated the same way society treats child abuse committed by adults. Peer abuse should be spelled out, including physical, verbal, emotional, and sexual harassment. Incidents should be reported, investigated, and resolved. The public, including children, should be familiar with reporting procedures and penalties should be widely publicized. Self-reporting could be required to take the pressure off of children who are afraid to disclose their abuse.

Parents and teachers must be tuned into the warning signs that indicate when certain children are bullying or being victimized. Olweus studies report that bullies are more aggressive toward peers and adults, have a more positive attitude toward violence, use violent means more than most students, are impulsive, have a strong need to dominate others, and express little empathy for the victim. Victims are more anxious and insecure than other students; are often cautious, sensitive, and quiet; commonly react by crying and withdraw when attacked by other students; suffer from low self-esteem; are lonely and abandoned at school; and can also be popular students who elicit the jealousy of others.

Parents, especially fathers, need to consider alternatives to physical violence when advising their children to deal with bullies. When physical force becomes the solution of choice on the playground, it continues to be an approach for dealing with all sorts of conflict in later years—inside and outside of family settings. Fighting is discouraged by all of the researchers and experts whose opinions we have read.

There is also a strong consensus among professionals that spanking sends the wrong message to children about the use of force to solve problems. There are many ways to enforce discipline—especially when children are young and eager for approval—that do not require physical contact to make a point. More and more parents are forsaking spanking and feeling confident about the use of alternative forms of instruction.

Verbal abuse must be recognized. It inflicts serious damage and plays a large role in escalating conflict to a more violent level. Students who have disabilities or special needs may require particular protection. Students need to hear that no one deserves to be harmed by teasing and that bullies who tease will be punished.

Emotional abuse should be discussed widely. Adults must be on the lookout for children who are isolated and ostracized. Recesses and birthday parties are frought with opportunities for children to cause their peers pain. When adults are sensitized to these problems, they can handle them adeptly and creatively but the awareness must come first. Many a parent who would never intentionally want to break the heart of a child might have done just that by not asking pointed questions when social activities are arranged. Such slights, which seem inconsequential to adults, are monumental for vulnerable children.

Adults need to be sensitive to their children's need for information about sexual development. When parents develop a comfort level in their conversations about sexuality, their children are not left to the mercy of playground "experts." Sexual harassment is a form of discrimination prohibited by Title VII of the Civil Rights Act of 1964 and Title IX of the Education Amendments of 1972. Recent research has determined that sexual harassment is rampant in elementary and secondary schools and parents should consider legal action when other attempts have failed.

Children need to learn how to manage their anger. They need to learn that everyone gets angry at times and it's okay to feel angry, but it's not okay to let it get out of control. There is a difference between what you feel and what you do. When anger is "stuffed" it can erupt at inappropriate times in inappropriate ways. There are techniques and skill training that can be offered to young people such as peer mediation systems and conflict resolution courses. They have become part of the curriculum in many schools and could be expanded even more.

During one all-male student focus group when I challenged the students to come up with creative ideas to stop bullying, a twelve-year-old suggested that we "pay kids to be nice to each other." The entrepeneurial spirit in America lives! When we consider what we spend on children who are "bad," the student's idea might be cost effective in the long run. I asked for a show of hands—"How many think that's a good idea? How many don't?" The vote was about half and half. The comments that followed are worth repeating.

Student #1: "The problem is if you pay a student $100 to be good for a week, what's to stop him from demanding $200 the next week and then he could get greedy and ask for $1,000 and so on and so on."

Student #2: "Somebody might act like they're being good just to get the money but they really wouldn't be any different."

Student #3: "If people are going to change, they have to change on the inside as well as the outside."

Student #4: "These guys are not being honest. I bet any one of them would change for $1,000."

Student #5: "People who really want to change don't do it for money."

An incentive system that doesn't involve money IS working at the McNair Elementary School in Hazelwood, MO. McNair is becoming a "fight-free" school, using a reward system of certificates, ribbons, and banners for their classroom door. If students are caught fighting they have to give up their ribbons and the banner is removed. Fights dropped from fifty-five per year before the program began to only three the following year. Workshops, activities, and projects are also part of the "Fight-Free" campaign.

There is still a major task for parents and teachers that bears serious attention. Adults must curtail the power of bullies. Peer-power issues are complicated and sometimes delicate because parents are, naturally, eager for their children to be popular. Students tell us that many bullies enjoy a certain amount of popularity because of the power they acquire and parents of bullies are not inclined to interfere when their children's currency is at stake. Adults must take responsibility and set limits for children who overstep reasonable boundaries and must empower the witnesses and victims to operate from strength.

Let's return to the theory of the concentric circles to illustrate.

A bully can:

1. Have an evaluation to determine if there is a physical or psychological basis for out of control behavior.
2. Learn ways to manage his/her anger. Sometimes it is not possible to control your thoughts or feelings but you can control your behavior and children can learn techniques that will work for them.
3. Learn to feel powerful without destroying someone else. True confidence and self respect can come from discovering a special talent, working hard to achieve a goal, taking a risk and succeeding—the list is endless.
4. Learn to be more empathetic, more concerned about the feelings of those who are victimized,
5. Develop social skills that will not alienate a bully from his or her peer group.
6. Report abuse that is happening and reach out to others for help.

The second circle represents the family.

The family can:

1. Ensure that family experiences create a positive, non-toxic atmosphere.
2. Be available and responsive to the child's wants and needs.
3. Transmit the important values we keep speaking about—anger control, respect for self and others, social skills and manners, empathy, responsibility.
4. Set limits and intervene when their bullying child is causing pain for another.
5. Impose and respect consequences that the school invokes.
6. Insist that their child apologize and make amends.

The school can:

1. Appoint a committee to determine clear, enforced policies against bullying that hold children accountable.
2. Create a weapon-free, safe environment for students and teachers.
3. Enlist everyone who has contact with students—bus drivers, custodians, cafeteria workers, nurses, counselors, principals, coaches—to be part of a consistent team that gives the same message: Bullying is unacceptable.
4. Be aware of signs of abuse in the home and make appropriate reports to authorities.
5. Bring peer abuse prevention curriculum, videos, speakers, and campaigns into the school structure.
6. Empower witnesses to defend victims, defuse bullies, and support each other; there is power in numbers.

7. Give children the attention, information, skills, and support they need.

The community can provide the sails or the jails. There can be recreation centers, religious activities, work and community service opportunities, caring neighbors, as well as child protection workers, mental health treatment facilities, and detention centers.

The culture as a whole can condone or check violence. It can value children or make them a low priority. It can offer them a sense of hope or it can reinforce feelings of worthlessness.

The case of Tony is a classic example of how all of these forces come into play. Tony was the youngest of four children and was abused and tormented by his siblings. Tony's mom, Elena, had a drug problem and neglected many of his emotional and material needs. Worse yet, she wasn't honest with him. She made promises she didn't keep and lied to him to cover up her addiction. When Tony started getting into fights at school, she defended him and took his side. Tony's behavior got more and more out of control. The fights and assaults became more brutal, which led to suspension from school, an eventual psychiatric hospitalization and ultimately a brief time in jail. The situation could easily have escalated into disaster if his mother hadn't been jolted into action because of a series of drive-by shootings committed by Tony's friends. These boys were headed for prison. Elena, like their parents, had always laughed off their exploits. It had always been someone else's fault, or they had been provoked, but they were never to blame. Elena was terrified that Tony was just one step away from the fate of his friends and she made a dramatic change in her behavior. It began when she stopped defending him, stopped blaming others, and insisted that he accept responsibility for his actions. She completely altered her attitude, her habits, her relationships. She became honest with herself, honest with her son, honest with the parents of her son's victims. She moved her family to a different neighborhood and enrolled Tony in another school. She talked and talked and listened and listened, concentrating mostly on the latter. Sometimes they cried together. This new relationship brought about a dramatic change in Tony. He reflected on the people he had met in the psychiatric unit, at his stay in jail, and took stock of his capabilities and opportunities. A girl with whom he was in love put him through an emotional wringer and out of his personal pain, he began to think about all of the people he had treated cruelly. He discovered poetry.

My conversation with Tony confirmed his mother's assessment. Tony looks back on his history as a bully with deep sorrow. He feels guilty about all the people he hurt and he cringes when he thinks of how "everyone was afraid of me." Life for him changed when his mother changed. He felt she was really concerned about him when she moved their family so he could go to a different school. When she stopped ignoring and excusing his behavior, he knew she really loved him. Tony believes that kids who get in trouble are kids who think that it doesn't matter what they do because no one cares. When others give up on them, they give up on themselves and life is meaningless. When Tony realized that someone cared, Tony began to respect himself.

Today he is a model student, making A's and B's, chairman of a class project to create a community garden, and writing stories and poems. A teacher in Tony's new school has turned him on to writing poetry, teaching him to tap into his own creative gift. It's a gift that helps him deal with his anger, his shame, and that fuels his dreams. But Tony will tell you that his greatest gift is a mother who loved him enough to transform herself and give him a new life.

This story is very special, not only because it illustrates such a remarkable conversion, but because it includes so many of the ideas we have been discussing, particularly the interdependence of the individual, the family, the school, the community, and the culture.

As we looked at some of the programs and curriculum that have been developed to help children cope, several approaches reoccurr. When organized in an anachronym they spell SCRAPES, which we hope can be prevented by the application of these principles.

S—Self esteem and social skills enrichment.

C—Conflict resolution and mediation skills.

R—Respect for differences, de-prejudicing exercises.

A—Anger management and assertiveness training.

P—Problem solving skills.

E—Empathy training.

S—Sexuality awareness training.

Some teachers have expressed resistance to adding anything to their overburdened teaching agenda. We do appreciate that teachers are expected to perform more and more of the roles that used to be the bailiwick of social workers and counselors. But it is for this very reason that SCRAPES must be added to the docket. The safety factor for teachers adds weight to this discussion. An article in the February 8, 1993, issue of *Time* Magazine claims that every school day 6,250 teachers are threatened with injury and 260 are actually assaulted. The National Center for Education Statistics reports 51 percent of public school teachers in the USA say they've been verbally abused, 16 percent have been threatened with injury and 7 percent have been physically attacked. Some examples of the problem that have appeared in newspapers:

- A seventh grader in New York was arrested for setting fire to his teacher's hair.
- Two middle school students in Ohio were charged with plotting to kill their English teacher with a 12-

inch fish-filleting knife while fifteen students placed bets on the plot.

- Seven sixth-grade students in Georgia planned to poison a teacher's iced-tea and trip her on the stairs because the students thought she was too strict.
- A substitute teacher in St. Louis died of a heart attack after being attacked by a fourth-grade student who didn't like the assignment the teacher handed out.
- Two other teachers in the Fall of 1995 were killed as as result of student attacks.

Teachers cannot teach in an atmosphere of fear and no educator deserves to feel threatened or concerned about personal safety.

The following programs that offer important prevention material have come to our attention:

- The Assist Program
- Bullyproof
- Bully-Proofing Your School
- Creative Conflict Resolution
- Kindness Is Contagious, Catch It!
- Let's Talk About Living in a World With Violence
- Project Essential
- Second Step
- Spreading Kindness
- Tough Kid Book
- What To Do When Kids Say "No"
- Sexual Respect Curriculum

THE ASSIST PROGRAM

The Assist Program is a series of nine books by Pat Huggins to promote students' growth in self-esteem, self-management, and interpersonal relationships. The books are filled with ideas and assignments for students that include role playing, drawing, puppetry, songwriting, crossword and find-a-word games, storytelling, partnering, interviewing, puzzles, pretests and posttests on lesson concepts, and a variety of approaches to keep children excited and interested while they are learning very specific skills. Assist was developed with Title IV-C Innovative Education Funds and was evaluated in second through sixth grade classrooms in four school districts. Statistically significant gains in self-concept and social skills occurred in eight out of nine assessments.

The nine books are:

Teaching Friendship Skills	
Primary Version	538 pages
Intermediate Version	606 pages
Helping Kids Handle Anger	516 pages
Helping Kids Find Their Strengths	714 pages
Building Self-Esteem in the Classroom	
Primary Version	602 pages
Intermediate Version	664 pages
Teaching Cooperation Skills	342 pages
Creating a Caring Classroom	582 pages
Teaching About Sexual Abuse	72 pages

The first eight books are $34.95 each. The last one is $17.95. They can be ordered from Sopris West, 1140 Boston Avenue, Longmont, Colorado 80501. Tel: 1-800-547-6747; fax: 303-776-5934; Internet http://www.sopriswest.com.

BULLYPROOF

Bullyproof is a teacher's guide on teasing and bullying for use with fourth and fifth grade students, developed by Nan Stein and co-authored with Lisa Sjostrom. The guidebook contains eleven sequential lessons. Class discussions, role plays, case studies, writing exercises, reading assignments, art activities, and nightly homework combine to give students the opportunity to explore and determine the fine distinctions between "joking," "teasing," and "bullying." Children gain a conceptual framework and a common vocabulary that allows them to find their own links between teasing and bullying and, eventually, sexual harassment. The guidebook encourages children to become researchers on bullying in their school, offering tips and questions. There are lessons on courage and rights and an excellent bibliography.

The sixty-page book is a joint publication of The Wellesley Center for Research on Women and the NEA Professional Library and can be ordered from the Center for Research on Women, Publications Department, Wellesley College, 106 Central St., Wellesley, MA 02181-8259. The cost is $19.95. Telephone: 617-283-2510; fax: 617-283-2504.

BULLY-PROOFING YOUR SCHOOL

Bully-Proofing Your School is a comprehensive approach to bullying prevention for elementary schools. It is the most complete curriculum contained in one book that we have been able to identify. The authors are Carla Garrity, Kathryn Jens, William Porter, Nancy Sager, and Cam Short-Camilli. The contents cover training for staff and students, and collaborating with parents. Some topics included are research findings, guidelines for intervention, effective communication instruction, conflict resolution, friendship skills, anger management, self-esteem, and multicultural issues. There is also a chapter on correcting errored thinking, based on the work of Dr. Stan Stamenow, a researcher on antisocial-personality development. This chapter has specific activities to work with aggressive children on "crooked" versus "straight" thinking, which Dr. Stamenow sees as a key factor in bully behavior.

There are 384 pages of group and individual activities, surveys, worksheets, role playing scenarios, and discussion guidelines. Included is a comprehensive Resource Guide that is divided into seven major sections: Videotapes and Films for Educators and Parents; Videotapes and Films for Students; Books for Educators; Books for Administrators, School-Based Teams, and Specialists; Books for Parents; Books for Primary Students; and Books for Intermediate Students. The cost is $29.95 and the book can be ordered from Sopris West, 1140 Boston Avenue, Longmont, CO 80501. Tel: 1-800-547-6747; fax: 303-776-5934; Internet http://www.sopriswest.com.

CREATIVE CONFLICT RESOLUTION

Creative Conflict Resolution is a paperback book by William J. Kreidler. The book includes more than two hundred activities for keeping peace in the classroom. The target population is kindergarten through sixth grade. The book is based on the model of a peaceable classroom where there are five qualities present: Cooperation, Communication, Tolerance, Positive Emotional Expression, and Conflict Resolution. Kreidler believes that conflicts are usually of three types: conflicts over resources, conflict of needs, and conflicts of values. The exercises, activities, and practice sessions specify age appropriate use. Included in the approach to conflict resolution is material covering communication skills, cooperative learning, and helping students handle anger, frustration, and aggression. An excellent section on Teaching Tolerance deals with physical disabilities, skin color, religious differences, political beliefs, and differences in beliefs and values.

Creative Conflict Resolution is a Good Year Book and can be ordered from your local bookseller or educational dealer. The book is 192 pages and sells for $12.95.

KINDNESS IS CONTAGIOUS, CATCH IT!

Kindness Is Contagious, Catch It! is a program guide for teachers and youth workers offered by the STOP Violence Coalition in Kansas City, Missouri. The guide takes a very positive approach to the problem of bullying and focuses on kindness. Four fun activities that deal with monitoring put-ups and put-downs, recognizing kind behavior, keeping a kindness calendar, and identifying adult role models who exemplify kindness are described. Volume II, of additional activities that teachers who have used the program have created, is also available. The learning skills that are emphasized are empathy, compassion, and respect. The target population for the material is elementary and middle school children, however, K through 12 students can be involved in the role model project. The program is very easy to incorporate and a twenty minute video training film is available. The program is being used in over 350 schools in the metropolitan Kansas City area and 32 states. It is praised by parents and school personnel in private, public, and parochial schools because of the ease with which it can be introduced. High school and middle school students can easily teach it to elementary school children as a "learning by teaching" project.

The program guide is 25 pages and costs $10.00. Volume II is also $10.00. Buttons and bumper stickers can be purchased for $1.00. There are price breaks for quantities. Contact: STOP Violence Coalition, 301 E. Armour, Suite 205, Kansas City, MO 64111. Tel: 816-753-8002; fax: 816-753-8056.

LET'S TALK ABOUT LIVING IN A WORLD WITH VIOLENCE

Let's Talk About Living in a World With Violence was written by James Garbarino, Ph.D. The book is written as a conversation guide and invites children to work together with other children and one or more adults. It handles a very disturbing topic in a way that is helpful and kind. It offers a number of activities that teach problem solving skills. Chapters include Where Can Violence Happen?—on TV,—In the movies,—In war,—On the streets,—At school,—At home. Children are encouraged to write stories, draw pictures, engage in peace practicing activities, and read. There are three pages of reading references.

A Guide for Parents and a Guide for Teachers, Counselors, and Other Professionals accompanies the forty-page activity book and is included in the $10.00 cost. Contact: Kathleen Kostelny, Erikson Institute, Suite 600, 420 North Wabash Avenue, Chicago, IL 60611.

PROJECT ESSENTIAL

Project Essential is a curriculum available to teachers in Kindergarten through Grade 8. This unique program seeks to develop responsible citizens whose behaviors, attitude, and values are reflective of four essential principles of effective human interaction: the positive use of errors, the appropriate roles of reason and emotion, the fulfillment of one's unique personal responsibilities, and the application of universal human rights. A controlled four-year experimental study involving over 3,000 students in public and private elementary schools found that students in classes using the *Project Essential* curricula had an enhanced ability and willingness to admit and correct mistakes, the ability to work without disrupting others, improved self-control, persistence in efforts to succeed at a task, and were better able to empathize with the needs and situations of others. Additional positive impacts included reduced physical aggression toward others; decreased tattling and bullying behaviors; diminished self-blaming and guilt; and fewer attention-getting episodes.

The curriculum, curricula-related products and supplies, *Teacher's Curriculum Manual* for individual grade levels, Teacher Training Video Kit, and other materials are available from: The Teel Institute for the Development of Integrity and Ethical Behavior, 101 East Armour Boulevard, Kansas City, MO 64111-1203. Tel: 816-753-2733; fax: 816-753-3193.

SECOND STEP

Second Step is a violence prevention curriculum that teaches skills to reduce impulsive and aggressive behavior in children. The materials, which are targeted for preschool through junior high, focus on empathy training, impulse control, and anger management. The curriculum is divided into four kits: Preschool–Kindergarten, Grades 1–3, Grades 4–5, and Grades 6–8. The content of the lessons varies according to the grade level and provides opportunities for modeling, practice and reinforcement of the new skills. The kits include lesson plans, a *Teacher's Guide*, Filmstrips-in-video lessons, laminated classroom posters, reproducible homework sheets, and a Family Overview video that introduces parents and caregivers to the very same skills their children are learning. A Family Guide contains everything a group facilitator needs to conduct six group meetings, including a thirty-minute overview tape, three skill training videos, a scripted facilitator's guide, masters of family handouts, and refrigerator magnets depicting the problem solving and anger management steps. There are Spanish supplements to the English language curricula for teachers who work with Spanish speaking populations. Student achievement tests showed that perspective-taking and social problem-solving skills improved significantly after children participated in the Second Step program.

Second Step Preschool-Kindergarten Curriculum $259

Second Step Elementary Curriculum Grades 1–3 $269

Second Step Elementary Curriculum Grades 4–5 $249

Second Step Middle School Curriculum
    Grades 6–8 $285

Client Support Services at Committee for Children can help with previewing, planning, ordering, and training information. Call 1-800-634-4449 between 8 A.M. and 5 P.M. Pacific Time. Or write to: Committee for Children, 2203 Airport Way S. Suite 500, Seattle, WA 98134-2027.

SPREADING KINDNESS: A PROGRAM GUIDE FOR REDUCING YOUTH AND PEER VIOLENCE IN THE SCHOOLS

Spreading Kindness is a program guide for elementary and middle schools. The guide contains over 150 activities divided into five sections:

1. Kindness activities
2. Cooperative learning and kindness activities
3. The Power of Positive Students (POPS) activities
4. Conflict Resolution activities
5. Activities for reducing bullying and put-downs.

The activities are arranged by grade level and also organized as classroom activities, all-school activities or small group counseling activities. *The Guide* is in an attractive, durable three-ring binder for easy use.

Prior to publication, *The Guide* was field-tested and evaluated in twenty-two elementary and middle schools in Colorado Springs.

The program guide is 200 pages, and the cost is $39.95 plus $5 shipping and handling. Available from The Kindness Campaign, c/o The C.U. Foundation, University of Colorado, Colorado-Springs, P.O. Box 7150, Colorado Springs, CO 80933-7150. Tel: 719-593-3446. Barry K. Weinhold, Ed.

THE TOUGH KID BOOK

The Tough Kid Book, written by Ginger Rhode, Ph.D., William R. Jenson, Ph.D., and H. Kenton Reavis, Ed.D., is written for both regular and special education teachers. The research-validated solutions included in this book help to reduce disruptive behavior in tough to teach students. *The Tough Kid Social Skills Book* and the Tough Kid Tool Box are complementary materials. The book is 120 pages and the cost is $19.50.

The Tough Kid Social Skills Book, written by Susan M. Sheridan, offers educators detailed, specific methods for assessing and identifying "Tough Kids" and teaching them appropriate social skills. The book provides theoretical background and practical strategies for maximizing the effectiveness of a social skills program, and presents practitioners with flexible outlines—each structured to be completed in less than sixty minutes, for conducting social skills sessions. Included are skills in social entry, maintaining interactions, and problem solving. The book is 230 pages and costs $19.50.

The Tough Kid Tool Box is an excellent companion piece to the *Tough Kid Book*. It contains all of the reproducible tools with step-by-step instructions, providing teachers with attractive, ready to use materials for managing and motivating Tough Kids. 214 pages. $15.95. All these resources are available from Sopris West, 1140 Boston Ave., Longmont, CO 80501. Tel: 1-800-547-6747; fax: 303-776-5934; Internet http://www.sopriswest.com.

WHAT TO DO WHEN KIDS SAY "NO"

What To Do When Kids Say "NO" is a teacher handbook that was developed by the Behavior Intervention Support Team of Ozanam Home for Boys in Kansas City, Missouri. It was created originally for students who were acting out, having problems in regular classrooms, and assigned to an alternative school environment but the material is now being requested by public schools for use with traditional students.

The B.I.S.T. believes that kids get in trouble because

- They don't know any better—Need: Information.
- They test limits—Need: Consistency.

- Can't manage feelings due to:
  Abuse/Neglect
  Organic/Neurological Problems
  Unattached/Unbonded Relationships

The philosophy behind this program is geared to helping children change their behavior. The emphasis is on protection rather than punishment. Punishment can work in the short run in that it can force cooperation, but it can also provoke passive-aggressive behavior and rage which later may be acted out destructively. People change when they are able to look at themselves and *own* their behavior. This is an extremely difficult and painful process. Safety and protection are stressed over and over again. The language teachers use is a major component of the program. When a child acts out, the teacher asks: "Are you okay?" "Can you sit in your desk even though I know it must be hard for you right now?" Is there any way I can help make it easier for you to sit down?"

A five-step Problem Solving Model provides a structure for helping children move from acting out to taking responsibility.

- Adults intervene when a child's behavior interferes with learning, threatens another person though disrespectful attitudes and actions, or is destructive to himself or others.
- A child who misbehaves faces the natural and logical consequences of his behavior
- Adults help the troubled child face his problems, understand his strong feelings, and take responsibility for his behavior.
- Adults problem solve with the child to determine appropriate ways to behave when experiencing strong feelings.
- Adults support the child as he works through the difficult process of confronting, owning, taking responsibility for, and changing his behavior.

This 64-page manual can be ordered from the Ozanam Home for Boys, 421 E. 137th Street, Kansas City, MO 64145; Tel: 816-942-5600. The cost is $20.00.

THE SEXUAL RESPECT CURRICULUM

The Sexual Respect Curriculum: Dealing with Sexism and Sexual Harassment with Intermediate School Students was written by Peter Miner to deal with sexism and sexual harassment for middle school students. The author teaches eighth grade at a public intermediate school in New York. The curriculum is divided into 11 lessons. Each lesson leads off with a question, such as: "Who are YOU? Would you rather get and give RESPECT or give and get FEAR?" or "Who are YOU? Are you a Sexual Harassment Perpetrator or Victim . . . or both?" Each lesson includes a survey, cartoon characters with captions, a discussion guide, and a log-writing assignment. Miner piloted his curriculum with his own students and used an attitude survey to test if male and female students who participated in the curriculum would exhibit a greater decrease in sexist attitudes and tolerance of sexually harassing behavior than students who had not been exposed. The results showed that both males and females in the experimental group had significantly altered their attitudes on the sexual harassment scale in a positive direction. The student comments on the curriculum were all positive and grateful for the opportunity to deal with issues of sexism and sexuality in a safe, learning atmosphere. The author is eager to have his curriculum used by other teachers in other school settings and age groups. *The Sexual Respect Curriculum* is 25 pages long and is available for $10.00 from Peter Miner, 247 Wadsworth Ave., #5W, New York, NY 10033. Tel: (212) 795-4003.

SUMMARY

There is a plethora of materials, curricula, videos, handbooks, and training materials described as violence prevention programs that can be found in catalogues, libraries, and other resource outlets.

Two catalogues that we have found helpful are: KIDS-RIGHTS, 10100 Park Cedar Drive, Charlotte, NC 28210; 1-800-892-KIDS; fax: 704-541-0113; and the Bureau for Violence Prevention (A subsidiary of NIMCO, Inc.), P.O. Box 9, 117 Highway 815, Calhoun, KY 42327-0009. Tel: 1-800-962-6662; fax: 502-273-5844. As we said before, we have only highlighted information that has come to our attention. We leave you to discover for yourself the resources that work best for you.

CHAPTER TWELVE

Challenges for Prevention

"Learning from the past, looking to the future."

IF CHILDREN, OUR "greatest natural resource," are our most troubled population, what must we do to ease their future? Too many children are hurting and too many children are hurting each other. The headlines plead with us to take action.

The most shameful aspect of the predicament is the way we distance ourselves from our children—as if we are almost fearful of catching their disease rather than committing to treat their ills. Today's children are a generation of alienated individuals and the world we bemoan will not change until we embrace them, whole-heartedly.

The African proverb, "It takes a village to raise a child," has become well known to all. But the village is in shambles. John Gardner speaks eloquently of community building in his treatise "National Renewal."

> Healthy families and communities give individuals the experi-
> ence of a life that extends beyond selfish interests. They are the
> arenas in which we learn responsibility to and for others. They
> provide individuals with a web of trust and social support that is

desperately needed in this transient, swiftly changing society. They combat personal insecurity with a simple, ancient message "You are not alone." When people are part of an effectively functioning community, they feel responsible in a way that isolated individuals never can.

It is clear that we must begin with the family, but where do we start? When the baby is born? Before the baby is born? With high school students who are imminent parents? With middle school students who are becoming parents in spite of our protestations? With elementary school students before they lose their innocence? Or with babies before they enter school with dysfunctional patterns? Maybe the best answer is "Yes," to all of the above.

During the course of this book, we have raised a lot of questions. Though we have offered many answers, there are many more that we "must grow into," as the poet Rilke advises.

If we could protect all children from abuse and neglect we would go a long way toward achieving a world in which every child received what all children deserve—to be cherished, respected, and taught the values and virtues that lead to a meaningful life. Programs that support parents of newborns, like Parents As Teachers, and parents of infants at risk for abuse, like Healthy Families America offer great promise in our dream to rebuild the village.

Two observations on this subject have guided my interest in this topic for the past twenty years.

The first one was made by Dr. Karl Menninger, the famed psychiatrist, in a speech he gave at a conference in Kansas in the late 1970s. He stated: "If we betray and abandon our children, their pain will turn to rage. Some of them will turn their anger inward and they will become depressed and suicidal. Others will turn their anger outward and they will become aggressive and homicidal. Consequently, our society will be spending most of its time and money building psychiatric hospitals and prisons." Dr. Karl, as he was affectionately known, was a remarkable visionary but even he could not possibly have imagined the billions of dollars that will be skimmed from our barren state resources to incarcerate more than a million of our citizens.

The other observation came from one of those incarcerated men. Back in 1978, when information about child abuse was scarce, Terry McClain, an inmate in the Kansas Correctional system, had a theory he pursued. Terry had been abused as a child and decided to survey the men on his maximum security cell block to check out his hypothesis that most prisoners had been battered when they were young. The results of his questionnaire were printed in a prison newsletter and he concluded with these words: "If you brutalize your children, don't ask any questions or wonder where you went wrong when they grow up into killers. If you allow your neighbor to brutalize his children, don't wail and gnash your teeth when those children grow up and kill yours."

Terry's statement is profound because it challenges us to care about the way *every* child is raised.

Keeping Our Schools Safe is the title of a 1995 nationwide survey commissioned by Honeywell Inc. about violence in schools. More than five hundred junior and senior high school teachers and students responded to a variety of questions about violence—its causes, impact, and possible solutions. More than 80 percent of the teachers and 50 percent of the students surveyed said providing classes for parents would be the most effective solution. Both teachers and students picked the breakdown of the family and media violence as two of their top three reasons for school violence. But students placed even more of the blame on peer influence, a factor most teachers rated very low.

The prevention of violence in our country is inextricably tied to the prevention of child abuse. Child abuse can be as devastating when it comes from the hands of a peer as when it comes from the hands of a parent. But, as we have stated before there are other influences beyond family that have an impact on peer abuse.

We have referred many times to the need for specific training in anger management. Parents are the most powerful teachers of managed or unmanaged anger. Most children will imitate what they learn in their homes, but children are turning elsewhere to acquire the skills parents failed to give them. Conflict resolution is not a panacea but it's very promising.

A number of years ago, we met a remarkable woman in Australia, Stella Cornelius, who envisioned a time in which using conflict resolution skills would be as common as reading. Cornelius' vision inspired me to capitalize on the success of programs like Coronary Pulmonary Resuscitation (CPR). In Kansas City, a campaign initiated by one of our greatest community philanthropists, Ewing Kauffman, trained a major segment of the population in the methods of CPR. Paula and I, along with hundreds of thousands of other volunteers completed four hours of training in a skill that we hope we will never have to use. If we could mobilize a similar effort to teach conflict resolution/negotiation skills to a large segment of the community, everyone who attended the seminar could use the skill. Lawyers, teachers, and others who practice mediation on a daily basis could transfer their skills to the community at large to our collective benefit.

The issue of weapons must be faced. Even though this subject stirs deep controversy, there must be agreement about limiting children's access to handguns. There are over 200 million guns in circulation in the United States. The World Health Organization tracks homicides in every country. In 1990, handguns were used to kill 13 people in Sweden, 91 in Switzerland, 87 in Japan, 68 in Canada, 22 in Great Britain, 10 in Australia, and 10,567 people in the United States. Even on a pro rata population basis, the U.S. record is shocking. Too many of those killings involved children. Where is our determination to stop the madness and restore the birthright of hope to our children?

Dr. Lenore Terr of San Francisco, an expert in childhood violence, states: "In studies of children who have been traumatized, the most striking finding is that they lose their optimism about the future. I think in this generation some kids unfortunately are not going to be making plans."

We cannot deny that racism is a factor in the inequities that lead to hopelessness, despair, and rage. Some people believe that attitudes determine behavior—to change behavior, we must first change attitudes. Others believe it may be impossible for some people to change their ingrained attitudes but at least laws can be put in place to guarantee certain rights, regardless of personal bias.

Prevention of prejudice based on race, religion, and gender has much greater prospects for success than reversing bigotry. In New Jersey, as reported by Ellen Graham, staff reporter of the *Wall Street Journal*, ". . . teachers have joined with law-enforcement officials in a systematic assault on hate matched in scope in few other states. In most of the state's 595 school districts, a subject loosely known as 'prejudice reduction' is beginning to take its place beside math and literature in the schools.

"The effort, locally controlled but encouraged by the state, encompasses everything from multicultural textbooks, cafeteria menus, and lessons on the roots and consequences of hatred."

The effort is laudable and appropriate. Data collected in the state indicates that 40 percent of the hate crimes in 1993 were committed by juveniles aged ten to seventeen. Graham continues: "Teachers say they are often at sea about how to handle acts of hate in school. The so-called Elizabeth Agreement, a 1993 memorandum of understanding between educators and prosecutors, codifies procedures. Under this agreement, school districts pledge to report suspected hate crimes to the police. They are also strongly encouraged to call police about noncriminal bias incidents, such as distributing neo-Nazi pamphlets. Dozens of New Jersey school districts have signed the document."

Further evidence of New Jersey's determination to confront prejudice is the state requirement to teach Holocaust education from kindergarten through twelfth grade. Plans are in place to expand the present curriculum to include genocides of Native Americans and other groups.

Family attitudes about race, religion, and gender will work their way into the thoughts and actions of the children who grow up in the home—be they messages of tolerance or intolerance. Schools then carry the burden of defusing the prejudice. On the one hand, we want our schools to turn out top academic achievers, superior in all subjects. On the other hand, we continually expect our schools to correct all the problems that stem from family life, or the lack of it. How can we place such an onus on the education system, beset as it is with such financial limitations and restrictions? Our cultural and spiritual institutions must join the effort to oppose racism in all its forms.

Violence in the media has been highlighted by both students and teachers as a root cause of student violence.

Leonard Eron has chaired the American Psychological Association Commission on Violence and Youth. He has conducted extensive research on the topic of how children learn aggression and has concluded that "All types of aggressive behavior, including illegal behaviors and criminal violence, had highly significant associations with exposure to television violence."

An interesting study was conducted in a remote Canadian community that did not have access to television until 1973. Social scientists took advantage of the unusual situation to compare the behavior of children in this community with two similar towns that had had television for a long period of time. They monitored rates of inappropriate physical aggression among forty-five first and second graders. After two years of television, the rate increased 160 percent in both boys and girls, and in both those who were aggressive to begin with and those who were not. The rate in the two communities that had television for years did not change. Similar results occurred when two Indian communities in northern Manitoba were studied. Aggression increased with the availability of television.

Researchers at four U.S. universities conducted a 1.5 million dollar, year-long study financed by the cable television industry that was made public in early 1996. The study concluded that violence is pervasive on broadcast and cable television programs in the United States and that there are substantial risks of harmful effects from viewing television violence. One of the findings showed that perpetrators of violent acts on television were unpunished 73 percent of the time. "When violence is presented without punishment, viewers are more likely to learn the lesson that violence is successful."

Movies that contain gratuitous violence are powerful forces in the culture, too. An article in *The New York Times* reported that recent popular movies include the following number of deaths: *Total Recall*—74, *Robocop 2*—74, *The Wild Bunch*—89, *Rambo 3*—106, *Die Hard 2*—264.

Between the seventh and twelfth grades, the average teenager listens to 10,500 hours of rock music, just slighlty less than the entire number of hours spent in the classroom from kindergarten through high school. Most adults don't listen to their children's music. If they did, they would be appalled by the messages of some of the current rock group recordings.

Any discussion of media violence must include video games that encourage children to chop off the rival's head, or rip out his backbone. Amputating limbs, decapitating and impaling heads, drilling necks to drain blood are the "skills" needed to win on some of the most popular computerized games. Monopoly and Scrabble are a far cry from the games of today that exalt violence, cruelty, and dismemberment.

Efforts to remove the MTV cartoon "Beavis and Butt-head" were initiated when a five year-old Ohio boy started a fire that killed his two-year-old sister. The boy's mother said he had become fascinated with fire after watching "Beavis and Butt-head." The two characters model other behaviors as well, such as torturing animals and using profanity. The petition drive prompted this response from a well-known TV critic: "Listen, we've got to lighten up on this Beavis and Butt-head thing. We're a nation having a hissy fit over cartoon characters. . . . Kids like these guys because they will do or say anything. But they are funny. Frog baseball. Frying insects at Burger World. Spray-painting dogs. . . . The world will soon discover that Beavis and Butt-head is just a fad. Then we'll miss these shameless bags of atrophy." The television critic's attitude is a reflection of our persistent willingness to ignore the implications of media violence.

The concept of media literacy is a new approach on the horizon that is a non-censorship strategy. Its purpose is to help children and youth acquire critical viewing skills—to examine what they are seeing, to distinguish between fantasy and reality, to consider the consequences of acts of violence, and to explore alternatives to violence as the solution to conflict. Whitney Vanderwerff, Director of the National Alliance for Non-violent Programming reports that "Beyond Blame," an effective program that can be used at home and in schools, is available through the Center for Media Literacy in Los Angeles, California.

Courage deserves a special heading as we pull all of the important ideas and pieces together. Knowledge without courage is impotent. We can bring reams of information to young people and adults but one student, one parent, one teacher at a time must be courageous in action to challenge the apathy.

There was a time when the younger generation and the adult population held divergent views of life and immortality. Young people were known for their view of life as indestructible while adults were more keenly aware of life's fragility. Fear of violence has brought the two groups much closer together in perspective and in search of leadership.

When Paula was about eight-years-old, she came home from Sunday school one day and told her father and me that she had learned the story of Moses. The lesson she had been taught about Moses emphasized the fact that Moses had led his people through the desert for forty years, but did not live to enter the Promised Land with his followers. The teacher used the story to illustrate the punishment Moses received because he lost his temper. I thought this was a rather a harsh interpretation of the story so I sought the counsel of a dear friend and mentor, Rabbi Gershon

Hadas. Rabbi Hadas listened thoughtfully to my recap of Paula's lesson and then shared his commentary on the moral of the Moses story. The lesson to be learned from Moses is that no one who takes on an enormous challenge is meant to see the beginning, the middle, and the end of their dream within their lifetime. Some of us, Rabbi Hadas said, will be involved in the initiation of dreams, some of us will struggle to keep dreams alive, and some of us will see dreams come to fruition. Those of us who begin a journey must be prepared to transmit our dream to those who follow.

In 1987, a distinguished group of clinicians, researchers, and educators gathered at the Schoolyard Bully Practicum, convened at Harvard by the National School Safety Center. These experts from around the world identifed five central ideas that need to be addressed to prevent bullying.

1. School bullying is a significant problem.
2. Fear and suffering are becoming part of the everyday lives of victims of bullying, making them avoid certain areas at school, stay home from school altogether, run away and, in isolated cases, commit suicide.
3. Young bullies are more likely to become criminals when they reach adulthood and to suffer from family and professional problems. Practicum participants strongly believe early prevention or intervention programs can not only stop school bullying, but also can save victims, the bullies and society from years of potentially tragic problems.
4. The prevailing attitude that kids fighting each other is a manifestation of normal youthful aggressive behavior must be discarded.
5. The United States should follow the lead of Japan and Scandinavia, whose governments have addressed bullying problems with national interven-

tion and prevention programs. Their efforts have
been successful in reducing bullying incidents and
can work in the United States as well.

Almost ten years later we continue to be guided by the
clarity of their vision. Increasing rates of violence among peers
compel us to continue to build on the groundwork laid by these
experts nearly a decade ago.

Dan Olweus, professor of psychology at Bergen University,
who chaired the Harvard conference continues to be a pas-
sionate spokesman for the cause. The longitudinal studies of
Leonard Eron, Ph.D., and Rowell Huesmann, Ph.D., linking
bullying behavior to criminal action are invaluable. Dr. Eron,
now Research Scientist and Professor of Psychology at the Institute for Social Research at the University of Michigan, has
also conducted research the results of which irrefutably connect
media violence to aggression in children. Robert Selman,
Ph.D., is doing some interesting work with students, pairing aggressive and non-aggressive students as a strategy to reduce bullying. Ron Slaby, Ph.D., Harvard psychologist is a strong
supporter of non-aggressive responses to bullies, promoting ne-
gotiation as an alternative to fighting. David Perry, Ph.D., professor of Psychology at Florida Atlantic University, is replicating
the Olweus study in the United States. John Lochman, Ph.D.,
Duke University Medical Center, is teaching bullies assertiveness instead of aggressiveness. Nathaniel Floyd, Ph.D., psychologist for the Board of Cooperative Educational Services of
Southern Westchester, N.Y. county, has set up individual and
group counselling services for bullies. Kenneth Dodge, Ph.D.,
and John Coie, Ph.D., continue to conduct research examining
the characteristics of bullies and victims. Delwyn Tattum and
David Lane, wrote the first book on the topic in 1989, *Bullying
in Schools*, about bullying in the United Kingdom. Bill Head,
whose bullied son, Brian, committed suicide because of bullying

and Tom Brown, who has created a videotape called "The Broken Toy," have joined forces to launch a national campaign to enact federal legislation to prevent physical and verbal abuse of young people by their peers. Ronald D. Stephens, Executive Director of the National School Safety Center (NSSC), is an eternal champion for the protection of children and offers the NSSC as a central clearinghouse for any of our readers who would like to communicate policies and programs that work, information that would be helpful to the field, and groups that are willing to take on the prevention of bullying as a major priority. As more and more people choose to become involved, coordination will be essential if we want to leverage our energy. The NSSC address is Pepperdine University, Malibu, CA 90263. Tel: 805-373-9977. The Center is a partnership of the U.S. Department of Justice, U.S. Department of Education, and Pepperdine University.

There is much work to be done! It is no sin to attempt and fail but it would be sinful to fail to make the attempt. A place to begin is the recommendations of prominent leaders and researchers in this field. They are very clear that bullying is a serious problem that demands public attention and affects millions of children. It disrupts the lives of the bullies who develop destructive behavior patterns, victims who suffer hidden as well as obvious wounds, and bystanders who witness the tyranny of their peers.

We believe that bullying, along with sibling abuse, should be viewed in the context of child abuse. The same legal, medical, psychiatric, social, and educational intervention concerns should be applied. Perpetrators should be held accountable and, when appropriate, treated.

Bullying behavior is one of the first symptoms of family breakdown and should be seen as a warning sign of violence to come—a red flag for timely intervention.

Power is a core component of the bullying issue. As John Gardner says: "The simple rule is: Hold power accountable.

Wherever it lodges!" This holds true for children as well as adults. Power equity for our children is essential. Bullies who abuse power must be challenged. At the same time, victims and witnesses must be empowered to carry out the idea that *cruelty is unacceptable.*

The comprehensive nature of the problem envelops all of us—as individuals, family members, and part of the community. There is a kind of sink-or-swim interdependence about this problem. Like the proverbial lifeboat, if a leak springs in one section of the raft everyone is in danger of drowning.

Prevention of bullying should be our highest priority because we will never have enough resources to correct the problems that we neglect.

We are grateful for the pioneer researchers who had the foresight to set up longitudinal studies that have given us valuable information, although more research is needed. There are no conclusive statistics about the extent of bullying and there are some contradictions about the profiles of bullies and victims. We agree that there are proactive and reactive bullies and passive and provocative victims, but we also believe that some bullies and victims are interchangeable. Not all victims lack esteem. Even popular, confident students become targets of bullying, and behind the bravado of many bullies is a frightened, insecure child.

Beyond that, however, there is much to be learned about what efforts work and which ones don't. Oprah Winfrey has highlighted bullying on several programs and has played a major role in stirring public interest on the topic and offering effective solutions. *Welcome to the Dollhouse,* an award-winning film, is adding new dimensions to public awareness and concern.

It would also be helpful for any future litigation if information about current and past cases of bullying and peer harassment in various jurisdictions could be collected for reference and citation. Legal research of this nature would be extremely valuable.

In the meantime, we offer the following specific recommendations.

Individual:
1. Early screening and testing for physical problems that can mark children for special attention and possible victimization.
2. Counseling for children who are either bullies, victims, or both.
3. Training for children in social skills, anger management, empathy, and conflict resolution.
4. Sensitizing adults and children to the power of words and use of language for harmful ends.

Families:
1. Access programs and support services such as Parents as Teachers and Healthy Families America.
2. Create nurturing environments where every child is valued and feels safe.
3. Teach respect for siblings and animals.
4. Serve as role models for their children in life skill management.
5. Monitor their children's diet of television, movies, video games, and music that present gratuitous violence without any consequences for perpetrators and victims.
6. Emphasize family activities that encourage non-violent behaviors.

Schools:
1. Every school principal should appoint a Council or Committee composed of parents, teachers, students, administrators, and bus drivers to develop policies that clearly define and enforce unacceptable

behavior. A bully, a victim, and a witness should be included on the Committee. Student Councils could have a role, as well.

2. Curriculae should be introduced that emphasizes social skills and self-esteem, conflict resolution, respect for others, assertiveness and anger management, problem solving, empathy, and sexual harassment protection.

3. Power must be lodged in the hands of accountable adults who are committed to equity power for children.

4. Every school should be a weapon-free environment.

5. Students should be given opportunities to perform community service as part of their school assignments.

6. Teachers must be given special training to handle their own responses to conflict as well as to assist students in mediating problems.

7. Safety and protection must be a high priority for everyone on school premises.

Community:

1. Safe neighborhoods that are free of drug houses, gangs, drive-by shootings, and all forms of violence which make children feel vulnerable and hopeless.

2. Legislation that outlaws the use of handguns by minors and prescribes severe punishment for adults who make such possession possible.

3. Prohibition of institutionalized prejudice or discrimination.

4. Advocacy groups committed to work for the prevention of child abuse, caused by adults and/or children.

Culture:

1. Media violence is voluntarily reduced.
2. Racism and sexism are replaced with acceptance and respect.
3. An ethical reawakening is fostered that values moral and spiritual tenets.

If cruelty, abuse, and harassment become the norm for our children, the future of our society is bleak, indeed. If every decision our society makes must answer the question,-in the tradition of the Hopi Indian Tribal Council—"Is it good for the children?" then our destiny will be secure. Nothing we do is more important than protecting our children—even from themselves.

Personal safety is the issue of the day. The solution will not be easy or quick, but if we don't address the root causes of violence now, we will be forced to spend even more dollars down the road. As someone put it, the real S & L crisis is not Savings and Loan, it's Sooner or Later! We are doomed to pay an indecent price for our indecent behavior . . .

> . . . Unless we honor the legacy of our shared humanity;
>
> . . . Unless we make deliberate, respectful choices every day;
>
> . . . Unless we ask the question: "What is the purpose of my life?" before it is too late to seek the answer.

Rabbi Hadas would urge us to carry the torch on this challenging journey, to muster the energy to continue without pause until we have passed the torch securely onto those who will commit to the dream.

APPENDIX A

Resources

American Dance Therapy Association
Patricia A. Gardner, Office Manager
2000 Century Plaza #108
10632 Little Patuxent Parkway
Columbia, MD 21044
410-997-4040

The Future of Children
David Finkelhor, Co-Director
Family Research Laboratory
University of New Hampshire
126 Horton Social Science Center
Durham, NH 03824
603-862-2761

James Garbarino, Ph.D.
Family LIfe Development Center
G-20 Martha Van Rensselaer Hall
Ithaca, NY 14853

Healthy Families America
National Committee to Prevent Child Abuse
Anne Cohn Donnelly, Executive Director
332 South Michigan Suite 1600
Chicago, IL 60604
312-663-3520

The Kansas City Star
1729 Grand Boulevard
Kansas City, MO 64108

The Learning Exchange
3132 Pennsylvania
Kansas City, MO 64111
816-751-4127
1-800-754-4414

Minnesota Department of Education
Sue Settel, Gender Equity Specialist
705 Capitol Square Building
550 Cedar Street
St. Paul, MN 55101

National Alliance for Non-violent
      Programming
Whitney Vanderwerff, Executive Director
1846 Banking
Greensboro, NC 27408
910-523-3325

National School Safety Center
Ronald D. Stephens, Executive Director
Pepperdine University
Malibu, CA 90263
805- 373-9977

Parents as Teachers National Center, Inc.
Mildred Winter, Executive Director
10176 Corporate Square Drive #230
St. Louis, MO 63132
314-432-4330

Sexual Harassment in Our Schools
Robert Shoop and Jack Hayhow
Allyn & Bacon
Simon & Schuster Education Group
160 Gould St.
Needham, MA 02195

When Children Abuse
The Safer Society Foundation Inc.
Linda Freeman-Longo, Executive Director
P.O. Box 340
Brandon, VT 05733
802-247-3132

Peer Abuse Survey Form

CHILD-TO-CHILD ABUSE HAS generally not been viewed am a cause for great concern among adults. But escalating youth violence in our society coupled with other social realities of our time call us to think anew about the potential impact of peer abuse. Perhaps childhood taunting and teasing falls on a continuum from "normal," non-harmful experiences to destructive, harmful experiences.

Do you agree with this? yes no

What do you think characterizes the difference between the two? _____

_____

_____

With regard to harmful, destructive experiences:

1. Can you recall any personal incidents of peer abuse (cruelty perpetrated against you by another child or children)? yes no

   If so, would you describe the abuse:

   a. physical—punching, poking, beating,

   b. verbal—tesming, namecalling, humiliating

    c. emotional—rejecting, isolating, terrorizing

    d. other _____

_____

2. At what age did the abuse occur? _____

3. What age was the perpetrator? _____   Male or female? _____

4. What kind of support did you receive, if any from other children or adults?

_____

_____

5. Would you please describe your most vivid memory of an abusive incident?

_____

_____

6. Looking back, did you ever treat another child or children in a way that you now think was harmful?

_____

_____

7. Have any of your clients ever recounted incidents of peer abuse?

What percentage?

a. child clients	0–25%	25–50%	over 50%
b. adult clients	0–25%	25–50%	over 50%

8. If you have children, did any of them experience any incidents of peer abuse?

_____

_____

9. Based on personal experience or your clients' experiences, do you think certain characteristics make children more vulnerable to abuse?   yes   no

   If yes, what are these?

   _____

   _____

   a. Personality attributes: fearful, shy, aggressive,   Other: _____

   _____

   _____

   b. Physical attributes: wearing glasses or braces, overweight, physical disability,

   illness,   Other: _____

   _____

   _____

Sample School Board Policy Prohibiting Harassment and Violence

Prepared by Minnesota School Boards Association   July 1993

I. GENERAL STATEMENT OF POLICY

It is the policy of Independent School District No. ___ (the "School District") to maintain a learning and working environment that is free from religious, racial or sexual harassment and violence. The School District prohibits any form of religious, racial or sexual harassment and violence.

It shall be a violation of this policy for any pupil, teacher, administrator or other school personnel of the School District to harass a pupil, teacher, administrator or other school personnel through conduct or communication of a sexual nature or regarding religion and race as defined by this policy. (For purposes of this policy, school personnel includes school board members, school employees, agents, volunteers, contractors or persons subject to the supervision and control of the District.)

It shall be a violation of this policy for any pupil, teacher, administrator or other school personnel of the School District to inflict, threaten to inflict, or attempt to inflict religious, racial or sexual violence upon any pupil, teacher, administrator or other school personnel.

The School District will act to investigate all complaints, either formal or informal, verbal or written, of religious, racial or sexual harassment or violence, and to discipline or take appropriate action against any pupil, teacher, administrator or other school personnel who is found to have violated this policy.

II. RELIGIOUS, RACIAL AND SEXUAL HARASSMENT AND VIOLENCE DEFINED

A. *Sexual Harrassment; Definition.* Sexual harassment consists of unwelcome sexual advances, requests for sexual favors, sexually motivated physical conduct or other verbal or physical conduct or communication of a sexual nature when:

  (i) submission to that conduct or communication is made a term or condition, either explicitly or implicitly, of obtaining or retaining employment, or of obtaining an education; or

  (ii) submission to or rejection of that conduct or communiction by an individual is used as a factor in decisions affecting that individual's employment or education; or

  (iii) that conduct or communication has the purpose or effect of substantially or unreasonably interfering with an individual's employment or education, or creating an intimdating, hostile or offensive employment or educational environment.

Sexual harassment may include but is not limited to:

  (i) unwelcome verbal harassment or abuse;

  (ii) unwelcome pressure for sexual activity;

  (iii) unwelcome, sexually motivated or inappropriate patting, pinching or physical contact, other than necessary restraint of pupil(s) by teachers, administrators or other school personnel to avoid physical harm to persons or property;

  (iv) unwelcome sexual behavior or words, including demands for sexual favors, accompanied by implied or overt threats concerning an individual's employment or educational status;

  (v) unwelcome sexual behavior or words, including demands for sexual favors, accompanied by implied or overt promises of preferential treatment with regard to an individual's employment or educational status; or

  (vi) unwelcome behavior or words directed at an individual because of gender.

B. *Racial Harassment; Definition.* Racial harassment consists of physical or verbal conduct relating to an individual's race when the conduct:

(i)   has the purpose or effect of creating an intimidating, hostile or offensive working or academic environment;

(ii) has the purpose or effect of substantially or unreasonably interfering with an individual's work or academic performance; or

(iii) otherwise adversely affects an individual's employment or academic opportunities.

C. *Religious Harassment: Definition.* Religious harassment consists of physical or verbal conduct which is related to an individual's religion when the conduct:

(i)   has the purpose or effect of creating an intimidating, hostile or offensive working or academic environment;

(ii) has the purpose or effect of subsantially or unreasonably interfering with an individual's work or academic performance; or

(iii) otherwise adversely affects an individual's employment or academic opportunities.

D. *Sexual Violence: Definition.* Sexual violence is a physical act of aggression or force or the threat thereof which involves the touching of another's intimate parts, or forcing a person to touch any person's intimate parts. Intimate parts, as defined in Minnesota Statutes Section 609.341, include the primary genital area, groin, inner thigh, buttocks or breast, as well as the clothing covering these areas.

Sexual violence may include, but is not limited to:

(i)   touching, patting, grabbing or pinching another person's intimate parts, whether that person is of the same sex or the opposite sex;

(ii) coercing, forcing or attempting to coerce or force the touching of anyone's intimate parts;

(iii) coercing, forcing or attempting to coerce or force sexual intercourse or a sexual act on another; or

(iv) threatening to force or coerce sexual acts, including thetouching of intimate parts or intercourse, on another.

E. *Racial, Violence; Definition.* Racial violence is a physical act of aggression or assault upon another because of, or in a manner reasonably related to, race.

F. *Religious Violence: Definition.* Religious violence is a physical act of aggression or assault upon another because of, or in a manner reasonably related to, religion.

G. *Assault Definition.* Assault is:
 (i) an act done with intent to cause fear in another of imme-
     diate bodily harm or death;
 (ii) the intentional infliction of or attempt to inflict bodily harm
     upon another; or
 (iii) to threat to do bodily harm to another with present ability
     to carry out the threat.

III.   REPORTING PROCEDURES

Any person who believes he or she has been the victim of religious,
racial or sexual harassment or violence by a pupil, teacher, administrator or other school personnel of the School District, or any person
with knowledge or belief of conduct which may constitute religious,
racial or sexual harassment or violence toward a pupil, teacher, administrator or other school personnel should report the alleged acts immediately to an appropriate School District official designated by this
policy. The School District encourages the reporting party or complainant to use the report form available from the principal of each
building or available from the School District office, but oral reports
shall be considered complaints as well. Nothing in this policy shall prevent any person from reporting harassment or violence directly to a
District Human Rights Officer or to the Superintendent.

A. *In Each School Building.* The building principal is the person responsible for receiving oral or written reports of religious, racial or
sexual harassment or violence at the building level. Any adult School
District personnel who receives a report of religious, racial or sexual harassment or violence shall inform the building principal immediately.

Upon receipt of a report, the principal must notify the School District
Human Rights Officer immediately, without screening or investigating the
report. The principal may request, but may not insist upon, a written complaint. A written statement of the facts alleged will be forwarded as soon
as practicable by the principal to the Human Rights Officer. If the report
was given verbally, the principal shall personally reduce it to written form
within 24 hours and forward it to the Human Rights Officer. Failure to forward any harassment or violence report or complaint as provided herein
will result in disciplinary action against the principal. If the complaint involves the building principal, the complaint shall be made or filed directly
with the Superintendent or the School District Human Rights Officer by the
reporting party or complainant.

B. *In the District.* The School Board hereby designates
_____ as the School District Human Rights Officer(s) to receive

reports or complaints of religious, racial or sexual harassment or violence. If the complaint involves a Human Rights Officer, the complaint shall be filed directly with the Superintendent.[1]

The School District shall conspicuously post the name of the Human Rights Officer(s), including mailing addresses and telephone numbers.

C. Submission of a good faith complaint or report of religious, racial or sexual harassment or violence will not affect the complainant or reporter's future employment, grades or work assignments.

D. Use of formal reporting forms is not mandatory.

E. The School District will respect the privacy of the complainant, the individual(s) against whom the complaint is filed, and the witnesses as much as possible, consistent with the School District's legal obligations to investigate, to take appropriate action, and to conform with any discovery or disclosure obligations.

IV. INVESTIGATION

By authority of the School District, the Human Rights Officer, upon receipt of a report or complaint alleging religious, racial or sexual harassment or violence, shall immediately undertake or authorize an investigation. The investigation may be conducted by School District officials or by a third party designated by the School District.

The investigation may consist of personal interviews with the complainant, the individual(s) against whom the complaint is filed, and others who may have knowledge of the alleged incident(s) or circumstances giving rise to the complaint. The investigation may also consist of any other methods and documents deemed pertinent by the investigator.

In determining whether alleged conduct constitutes a violation of this policy, the School District should consider the surrounding circumstances, the nature of the behavior, past incidents or past or continuing patterns of behavior, the relationships between the parties involved and the context in which the alleged incidents occurred. Whether a particular action or incident constitutes a violation of this policy requires a determination based on all the facts and surrounding circumstances.

In addition, the School District may take immediate steps, at its discretion, to protect the complainant, pupils, teachers, administrators or

1. In some School Districts the Superintendent may be the Human Rights Officer. If so, an alternative individual should be designated by the School Board.

other school personnel pending completion of an investigation of alleged religious, racial or sexual harassment or violence.

The investigation will be completed as soon as practicable. The School District Human Rights Officer shall make a written report to the Superintendent upon completion of the investigation. If the complaint involves the Superintendent, the report may be filed directly with the School Board. The report shall include a determination of whether the allegations have been substantiated as factual and whether they appear to be violations of this policy.

V. SCHOOL DISTRICT ACTION

A. Upon receipt of a report, the School District will take appropriate action. Such action may include, but is not limited to, warning, suspension, exclusion, expulsion, transfer, remediation, termination or discharge. School District action taken for violation of this policy will be consistent with requirements of applicable collective bargaining agreements, Minnesota and federal law and School District policies.

B. The result of the School District's investigation of each complaint filed under these procedures will be reported in writing to the complainant by the School District in accordance with state and federal law regarding data or records privacy.

VI. REPRISAL

The School District will discipline or take appropriate action against any pupil, teacher, administrator or other school personnel who retaliates against any person who reports alleged religious, racial or sexual harassment or violence or any person who testifies, assists or participates in an investigation, or who testifies, assists or participates in a proceeding or hearing relating to such harassment or violence. Retaliation includes, but is not limited to, any form of intimidation, reprisal or harassment.

VII. RIGHT TO ALTERNATIVE COMPLAINT PROCEDURES

These procedures do not deny the right of any individual to pursue other avenues of recourse which may include filing charges with the Minnesota Department of Human Rights, initiating civil action or seeking redress under state criminal statutes and/or federal law.

VIII.   HARASSMENT OR VIOLENCE AS ABUSE

Under cerain circumstances, alleged harassment or violence may also be possible abuse under Minnesota law. If so, the duties of mandatory reporting under Minn Stat. §626.556 may be applicable.

Nothing in this policy will prohibit the School District from taking immediate action to protect victims of alleged harassment, violence or abuse.

IX.   DISSEMINATION OF POLICY AND TRAINING

A. This policy shall be conspicuously posted *throughout* each school building in areas accessible to pupils and staff members.

B. This policy shall appear in the student handbook.

C. The School District will develop a method of discussing this policy with students and employees.

D. This policy shall be reviewed at least annually for compliance with state and federal law.

Multicultural and Gender-Fair Curriculum Rule,

Minnesota State Board of Education

Minnesota Rules Part 3400.0SSO

Subpart 1. Establishment of a Plan

The school board in each district shall adopt a written plan to assure that curriculum developed for use in district schools establishes and maintains an inclusive educational program. An inclusive educational program is one which employs curriculum that is developed and delivered so that students and staff gain an understanding and appreciation of:

A. the cultural diversity of the United States. Special emphasis must be placed on American Indians/Alaskan Natives, Asian Americans/Pacific Islanders, Black Americans, and Hispanic Americans. The program must reflect the wide range of contributions by and roles open to Americans of all races and cultures.

B. the historical and contemporary contributions of women and men to society. Special emphasis must be placed on the contributions of women. The program must reflect the wide range of contributions by and roles open to American women and men.

C. the historical and contemporary contributions to society by handicapped persons. The program must reflect the wide range of contributions by and roles open to handicapped Americans.

Subpart 2. Specifications for the Plan
The current plan must:

A. address the manner in which the multicultural and gender-fair concepts in Subpart 1, items A, B, and C, are to be incorporated into the curriculum goals, learner outcomes, and evaluation processes established in the district;

B. determine the extent to which the district curriculum advisory committee established by Section 126.666, Subdivision 2, will be involved in implementing this part;

C. include evidence of substantive involvement by women, persons of color, and handicapped persons in the development of the plan. In communities with no persons of color, the district shall utilize resource people available in the region, state, or nation whenever the plan is developed, reviewed, or revised;

D. include specific goals, objectives, and implementation timelines for the curriculum processes, content, and materials needed for each of the areas in Subpart 1.

E. include procedures for systematic monitoring and evaluation of the plan; and

F. include a description of the program planned to inservice all staff in the areas related to Subpart 1, items A, B, C, and Subpart 2, items D and E.

Subpart 3. Filing, Reports, Review, and Revision

A. The current plan must be on file in the administrative offices of the district and with the Commissioner of Education.

B. The district shall submit status reports on implementing the current plan as requested by the Commissioner.

C. The current plan must be reviewed at least every six years and be revised as necessary.

Effective Date
Minnesota Rules, part 3500.0550, is effective June 1, 1990. The plan required to be adopted under Subpart 1 must be adopted before that date and must be in effect and on file in the district and with the Commissioner of Education by that date.

Adopted by the Board on December 13, 1988.
Final version approved for printing in the State Register of flay 30, 1989.

127.455   MODEL POLICY.

The Commissioner of education shall maintain and make available to school boards a model *religious. racial. and* sexual harassment and violence policy. The model policy shall address the requirements of section 127.46.

Each school board shall submit to the commissioner of education a copy of the *religious. racial. and* sexual harassment and sexual violence policy the board has adopted.

APPENDIX E

Harassment and Violence Policy

Minnesota Statute 127.46

Each school board shall adopt a written sexual, religious and racial harassment and violence policy that conforms with [human rights statute). The policy shall apply to pupils, teachers, administrators, and other school personnel, include reporting procedures, and set forth disciplinary actions that will be taken for violation of the policy. Disciplinary actions must conform with collective bargaining agreements and [fair discipline and fair dismissal policies].

The policy must be conspicuously posted throughout each school building, *given to each district employee and independent contractor at the time of entering into the person's employment contract*, and included in each school's student handbook on school policies. Each school must develop a process for discussing the school's sexual, religious and racial harassment and violence policy with students and school employees.

As amended - 1994

Acknowledgments

I KNEW THAT I was going to have to channel this passion of mine about child cruelty into a task—advocacy, programming, or perhaps training, but the possibility of a book might never have surfaced if it hadn't been for Charles Mallory, a friend and literary agent in Kansas City. He prodded, guided, and encouraged me to write about this topic and connected me to Deborah Shouse to help me get my sea legs as an author. He also suggested that I co-author this book with a psychologist which led to an extraordinary partnership with my daughter, Paula. I have often stated that "I just want to be like Paula when I grow up," and that is still my goal. When she was a teenager, I was in awe of her maturity and amazing ability to do so many things so well. My respect and affection for her is unbounded and I will miss sharing the time and the task that our book demanded.

Another important link in the chain of this book being published is Irving Sloan, a college friend of my husband's and a legendary middle-school teacher in Scarsdale, New York. He not only validated the relevance of our book about bullies and victims, he put us into the hands of Michael Cohn, our literary agent, for which we will be forever grateful. Michael, in turn, delivered us to "one of the best in the business," Betty Anne Crawford, our editor at M. Evans and Company, Inc. Betty Anne more than lived up to her advance notices and "edited" us with lavish amounts of patience and wisdom.

Joanne Greenberg, a talented author and cherished friend, served as a "reader," and Carol Hillman, an author as well, has been an invaluable mentor.

Our niece, Jennifer Weissman, volunteered to do some research for us and Emily Berkley fine-tuned the research role. Carole Lander, our cousin and an esteemed school counselor, made it possible for me to work with teachers, parents, and students who provided a number of indelible anecdotes for our book, as did Brenda Randel, a middle-school principal. Linda Dupree, a remarkable high-school teacher, allowed me to interact with students of hers whose follow-up letters were poignant, on target, and posed many dilemmas for consideration. Penni Holt, an educational psychologist and longtime friend of ours, critiqued our work and gave us astute advice, which we followed.

The STOP Violence Coalition served as a nest where many of the ideas and experiences related in this book incubated. Through this special organization I had opportunities to work with thousands of students who gave me invaluable insights over the past five years. I am especially grateful to Polly Runke and Barbara Unell who share our commitment to bring more kindness into children's lives. Katie Nealy and Ryan Baber are high-school students who became cherished friends when they were in first grades and served as consultants on many of the issues that we explored. Bev Sheldon was an invaluable sounding board and Ruth Forman made two indispensable contributions to this book. Jeanine Albanese and Bob Goodman contributed crucial typing when it was needed most.

I would especially like to thank Greg Musselman and inmates at the Lansing Correctional Facility who eagerly shared personal stories to help us illuminate the problem.

The Holiday Inn in Manhattan, Kansas, was the meeting place between Salina (Paula's home) and Kansas City (my home) where we lugged our boxes of "stuff" and did our major collaborating. The gracious staff let us spread our papers all over their lounge area, hovered over us like midwives, and never doubted that we were doing lifechanging work.

Becoming a writer while continuing my full time role as child advocate and community volunteer was very stressful at times. Fortunately, I am blessed with a generous supply of energy and even more blessed with family and friends who not only accommodated my needs but never made me feel guilty for the times I didn't meet theirs. Friends eagerly became my clipping service, cheerleaders, and support group on retainer.

My sons, Jeff and Marc, never bullied their classmates. On many occasions they reached out to rejected classmates and behaved with a sensitivity they have carried into adulthood. They have brought me great pride, treasured daughters-in-law, and spectacular grandchildren. Paula's husband and children are equally adored.

My husband has always been there for me in every challenge I have ever attempted. A dear friend once used the metaphor of a tether ball to describe our relationship—my husband being the steady, sturdy pole while I, the ball, could spin out into the universe, safely fastened to some measure of reality by the constancy of his affection and strength. In this bookwriting challenge, he not only shared our computer and rescued me from a number of computer crises; he shared an office with me, which no orderly person should ever have to do! His humor and his love have made all things possible for me.

—*SuEllen Fried, A.D.T.R.*

Just as we think of children and bullies and victims as living in the midst of contextual concentric circles of family, community, and culture, I want to acknowledge my own location in a contextual environment of layers of tremendous support and encouragement. I am grateful to be living in a political and social climate that encourages questioning, and I am fortunate to live in Salina, Kansas, a small and spirited community where people are good to each other and see it as their obligation to create the quality of communal life they desire and deserve.

Many, many friends make up my community of spirit, and each of them challenges and nurtures me in immensely important ways. I want to specifically acknowledge two very special friends and colleagues. Jayna Halverson, Ph.D., and Jay Bevan, Ph.D., have been cherished companions on the journey of professional development. They both read early drafts of this manuscript and raised important questions in their comments.

My family is my richest blessing of all. My brothers Jeff Fried and Marc Fried provided my first venue for exploring the peaks and valleys of sibling relationships. Their teasing was great preparation for life, and I treasure their wit and humor and respective talents.

I wish that every female on earth had a father like mine, Harvey Fried. My understanding of the power of the gifts he gave me deepens with each passing year. His assumption that I would make an important contribution to my community afforded me the luxury and privilege of taking myself seriously as a matter of course, and, in a complete departure from his usually rigorous criteria for achievement and demanding standards for success, he always thought I was the best at every dance class, school play, and social situation. His steadfast commitment to my mother's personal and professional development registered deeply, and taught me to expect remarkable things from my spouse and marriage.

My mother, and co-author, has given me more than anyone could ask, and often more than I have deserved. Even our most difficult chapter together resulted in wonderful gifts for me in terms of my independent sense of self. She has been an incredible model for me, loving her husband, children and grandchildren so completely while somehow managing to serve her community, maintain a rich and intricate web of relationships, and nurture and sustain her own passions. She gives unendingly, and her invitation to help her with this book is another one of many, many ways that she has always provided me with profoundly important opportunities.

My three children, Elise, Allison, and Sam, are at the center of my involvement in this book. Like other parents who will read this book, I want nothing more than to make the world a safe, supportive place for them. This material has been painful to face at times, but my children remind me that I need to confront these issues so that I can help them be better equipped to deal with the hardships that await them. I am grateful for the many times they were called upon to understand that other activities had to be delayed while I worked on this project.

Finally, I want to acknowledge my husband, Brad Stuewe. In our life together Brad has been unwavering in his support of my personal and professional growth, which not infrequently places significant demands on him. In this, as in many other projects, he has taken up slack in other places so that I could work. He has always pushed me to take the next step, quite often long before I have felt ready to do so. He is my closest friend, my honest critic, and my greatest source of comfort, and I am tremendously grateful to share my life with him.

—Paula Fried, Ph.D.

Index

acknowledgments, 209–213
ADHD (Attention Deficit Hyperactive Disorder), 88, 97
Adler, Eric, 68
adult intervention, 129–150
  as community advocates, 147–150
  counseling children about emotional abuse, 53–54
  educating children about sexual harassment, 69–70
  helping children deal with anger, 115–117, 133, 153–154
  with other parents, 138–139
  with others children, 137–138
  with own children, 130–137
  recommendations for verbal abuse, 42–43
  setting limits for bullies, 155
  sex education for children, 64–65, 66, 70, 153
  in sibling abuse, 74–76, 79–83
  with teachers and school administrators, 139–143
  teachers with students, 143–147
  See also peer intervention
age
  of juvenile sexual offenders, 62
  put–downs and, 39–40
  rites of passage and, 25–27
  and sex of aggressive children, 6
  of victims, 10

age *(continued)*:
  youth violence and, 17–19, 21
aggression
  accepting in children, 78–79
  behavior acceptable in boys, 13–14
  increases in, 17–19
  learning patterns of, 89
  parenting styles and, 89–90
  reactive and proactive, 88
  in schools, 24–25
  television and increasing, 178–179
  types of bullies and, 87–88
  See also physical abuse *and* violence
aggressive responses to bullies, 113
American Association of University Women, 60
anger
  books about, 161
  defusing with hugs, 119–120
  helping children deal with, 116–117, 133, 153–154
  identifying problems with, 115
  learning to control, 23–24
"Anger is all the Rage" (Ostrom and Moriwaki), 114
assertive responses to bullies, 113
assertive training, 132–133
Assist Program, 160–161

Attention Deficit Hyperactive Disorder (ADHD), 88, 97

Battered Child, The (Kempe and Helfer), 31–32
Battered Woman, The (Walker), 24
Behavior Intervention Support Team, Ozanam Home for Boys, 168–170
Bergman, Stephen, 56
Berry, Joy, 114
"Beavis and Butt-head," 179–180
bickering between siblings, 79
biological basis for violence, 24
Bishop, Ann, 119
Blumberg, Neil, M.D., 20
books and curricula on bullying prevention, 161–171
boys
    acceptable aggressive behavior for, 13–14
    as bullies, 21, 94
    effect of sexual abuse on, 60
    father's approval of fighting and, 21–22, 133, 152
    See also gender *and* girls
brainwashing techniques, 37
"Broken Toy, The," 183
Brown, Tom, 183
Building Self-Esteem in the Classroom (Huggins), 161
bullies, 85–95
    ages of aggressive children, 6
    cognitive patterns of, 90–91, 161–163
    confronting, 122–124
    cultural influences on, 104
    family influences on, 103
    gender and, 6, 10, 21, 94–95
    goals for, 155
    interviews with, 92–94
    learning to control anger, 23–24

bullies, *(continued)*:
    life experiences of, 88–90
    need for parental love, 130–131, 157–158
    physiological traits and, 88
    popularity of, 108
    as potential criminals, 91–92
    power and, 9, 31–32, 35–36, 127, 183–184
    reasons for becoming, 108–109
    relationship to violence, 152
    selecting victims, 97–98
    suggestions for self–awareness, 111–112
    types of aggression and, 87–88
    witnesses and, 110–111
    See also bullying *and* witnesses
bullying
    as abusive behavior, 5–6
    ages of victims of, 10
    consequences of, 10, 37–38
    effect of television on, 27–28, 29, 104, 178
    factors effecting, 6–9
    intervention strategies and, 101–102
    power and, 9, 31–32, 35–36, 127, 183–184
    preventing, 11–12, 107–128, 144–147
    racism and, 123
    school influences on, 103
    sexual harassment and, 61–62, 70
    stories from adults of, 9
    teasing distinguished from, 2–3, 9–10, 12
    See also bullies *and* bullying-prevention solutions
Bullying in Schools (Tattum and Lane), 182
bullying-prevention solutions, 11–12, 144–147, 151–171
    Assist Program, 160–161

bullying-prevention solutions *(continued)*:
books and curricula about, 161–171
challenges and, 173–187
education about bullying, 152–153
Federal laws and, 153
fight–free schools, 154
goals for bullies, 155
goals for families of bullies, 156
incentive programs, 154
parental love for children, 130–131, 157–158
problem solving models as, 169
recommendations, 185–187
resources for, 189
school programs, 156–157, 160
Schoolyard Bully Practicum guidelines, 181–182
teaching children about anger, 153–154
See also adult intervention; challenges; *and* peer intervention
Bullyproof (Stein and Sjostrom), 162
Bully-Proofing Your School (Garrity, Jens, Porter, Sager, and Short-Camilli), 162–163

Campbell, Joseph, 26
cartoons, 179–180
catalogues on violence prevention, 171
Catoni, Bonnie, 101
challenges
eliminating hate crimes, 177
handguns, 176
media violence, 178–179
protecting children from abuse and neglect, 173–175
racism, 123, 177
and recommendations, 185–187

children
assertive training for, 132–133
bullying-prevention recommendations for, 185
dealing with anger, 116–117, 133, 153–154
fear of being different, 135–137
forms of emotional abuse by parents, 46
identifying emotional abuse, 53–54, 134
identifying problems with anger, 115
locking into roles, 76, 77
need for parental love, 130–131, 157–158
protecting from abuse and neglect, 173–175
sexual abuse of, 55–56
teaching core values, 130–131
See also peer intervention
Children's Book About BEING BULLIED, A (Berry), 114
choosing team members, 145–146
Civil Rights Act (1964), 153
Clevenger, Bev, 140–141
Clore, Ellen R., 5
clothing and self–esteem, 121
cognitive patterns of bullies, 90–91, 162–163
Coie, John, 87–88, 90–91, 182
communities
bullying prevention and, 157, 186
community service programs, 126–127
influences on, 8
role of adult advocates in, 147–150
concern as abuse, 37, 42
conflict-mediation and -resolution programs, 102, 125, 142–143

consequences
  of bullying, 10
  of emotional abuse, 45
  of sexual abuse, 57–60
  of sibling abuse, 73–74
  of verbal abuse, 37–38
  for victims, 99–101
contact sexual abuse, 56, 58–60
Corneluis, Stella, 176
corruption, 52–53, 54
Creating a Caring Classroom (Huggins), 161
Creative Conflict Resolution (Kreidler), 163
cultural influences
  attitudes about violent behavior, 148–150
  on bullies, 8, 104
  bullying prevention and, 187
  on sexuality, 64–64
Cunningham, Carolyn, 62
curricula on bullying prevention, 161–171

Danbois, Doris, 101
Davis, Michael, 25
Deadly Consequences (Prothrow-Stith), 117–120
Detroit Lakes Junior High School, 66
differences and abuses, 135–137
disabled as victims, 34–35, 98–99, 135–136
Dodge, Kenneth, 87–88, 90–91, 182
"Down In the Zero" (Vachss), 45

education
  about anger, 23–24, 116–117, 133, 153–154
  about emotional abuse, 153
  about sex, 64–65, 66, 70, 153
  about verbal abuse, 153

education *(continued)*:
  empathy training, 134–135
emotional abuse, 45–54
  adults' memories of, 10–11
  as bullying, 10
  corrupting and, 52–53, 54
  defining, 46
  education about, 153
  intensity of, 46–47
  peer isolation and, 48–50
  rejecting as, 47–48
  symptoms of, 53
  teaching children to identify, 53–54, 134
  terrorizing and, 50–52
  types of, 45, 46, 53
  unworthiness and, 45
empathy training, 134–135
Erickson, Angie, 34–35
Eron, Leonard, 89, 91–92, 178, 182
errored thinking, 90–91, 162–163
Espeland, Pamela, 67
ethics of witnesses, 121–122, 124–125

Faber, Adele, 74
families
  attitudes of tolerance in, 178
  breakdown of, 173–175
  family members as bullies, 92
  father's approval of fighting, 21–22, 133, 152
  influence on bullies, 7–8, 103
  insulting members of, 39
  of juvenile sexual offenders, 62–63
  need for parental love, 130–131, 157–158
  role in preventing bullying, 156, 185
Faris, Nathan, 3–4
fight-free schools, 154

fighting
    pros and cons of, 117–120
    social pressure for, 21–22, 133,
        152
Finkelhor, David, 55–56
flirting, 67
Floyd, Nathaniel, 88–89, 182
fraternity hazing, 25–26, 29
Freeman-Longo, Rob, 62

Garbarino, James, 45, 53, 164–165
Gardner, John, 173–174, 183–184
Garrity, Carla, 162
gender
    of aggressive children, 6
    bullying and, 6, 10, 21, 94–95
    and effect of sexual abuse, 60
    gender–fair curriculum rules,
        203–205
    See also boys *and* girls
girls
    as bullies, 21, 94
    effect of sexual abuse on, 60
    peer pressure and adolescent, 26
    physical abuse from boyfriends,
        19
    See also boys *and* gender
Goffstown, New Hampshire, 100
Golding, William, 140
gossip, 38, 120–121
Graham, Ellen, 177
Guttmann, Edna, 45

Hadas, Rabbi Gershon, 180–181
Haley, Jean, 47–48
handguns, 19–20, 29, 176
Harassment and Violence Policy
    (Minnesota School Boards Asso-
    ciation), 61, 143, 195–201, 207
harmful words, 33–35
hate crimes, 177
Hayhow, Jack, 69

hazing, 25–26, 29
Head, Bill, 182–183
Helfer, Ray, Dr., 31–32
Helping Kids Find Their Strengths
    (Huggins), 161
Helping Kids Handle Anger (Hug-
    gins), 161
Hible, Judith A., 5
high–aggressive victims, 97
Honeywell, Inc., 175
horseplay, 13–14
"Hostile Hallways" (American Asso-
    ciation of University Women),
    60
Huesmann, Rowell, 89, 182
hugging, 119–120
Huggins, Pat, 160
Human Mind, The (Menninger), 135
humor, 40, 43, 133

incentive systems, 154
intensity and duration
    as sign of bullying, 9
    of verbal abuse, 35
intent to harm, 9
intervention
    adult, 129–150
    peer, 107–128
    strategies for, 101–102

Japanese teen suicides, 100
Jens, Kathyrn, 162
Jenson, William R., 167–168
juvenile sexual offenders, 62–63

karate, 119
Kauffman, Ewing, 176
Kaufman, Gershen, 113
Keeping Our Schools Safe (Honeywell,
    Inc.), 175
Kelly, Dennis, 121

Kempe, C. Henry, 31–32
Kindness Campaign, The, 167
Kindness Is Contagious, Catch It!
(STOP Violence Coalition), 164
Kinduris, Pauline Pauly, 101
Kreidler, William J., 163

Ladd, Gary, 98
Lane, David, 182
Larrabee, John, 101
lawsuits, 149, 150
*Let's Talk About Living in a World With
Violence* (Garbarino), 164–165
Lochman, John, 91, 182
Lord of the Flies (Golding), 140
loving children, 130–131, 157–158
low–aggressive victims, 96

MacFarlane, Kee, 62
Maiuro, Roland, 114–115
Mazlish, Elaine, 74
McClain, Terry, 175
media
involving in awareness of bul-
lying, 149
viewing literacy for, 180
See also television
mediation skills, 176
Menninger, Dr. Karl, 135, 174–175
Miner, Peter, 66, 170
Minnesota School Boards Association
Harassment and Violence Policy,
61, 143, 195–201, 207
Minuteman Regional Vocational
Technical High School, 66
Moriwaki, Lee, 114
Moyers, Bill, 26
mutuality, 56

National School Safety Center
(NSSC), 181–182, 183

negative feelings between siblings,
74–76
noncontact sexual abuse, 56, 57–58
NSSC (National School Safety
Center), 181–182, 183
Nuwer, Hank, 25

Olweus, Dan, 90, 96, 97, 152,
182
ostracization, 48–50, 53, 145–
146
Ostrom, Carol M., 114
"Overcoming Bullying Behavior"
(Clore and Hibel), 5
Ozanam Home for Boys, 168–
170

paranoia, 91
parents
accepting aggressive nature of
children, 78–79
comparing siblings, 76, 82
emotional abuse of children and,
46
handling sibling abuse, 74–76,
79–83
intervening with other parents,
138–139
intervening with others children,
137–138
intervening with own children,
130–137, 157–158
loving children who are bullies,
157–158
and parenting styles, 89–90
talking with teachers and school
administrators, 139–143
Parents Anonymous, 131
Parents as Teachers, 131
passive victims, 96, 102, 113
Patterson, Gerald, 90
Pauly, Megan, 101

peer abuse, 150
>   peer isolation, 48–50, 53, 145–146
>   peer pressure, 121
>   *See also* bullying *and specific types of abuse listed individually*
Peer Abuse Survey Form, 191–193
peer intervention, 107–128
>   with conflict-mediation and -resolution programs, 102, 125, 142–143, 151–150
>   creative responses to bullies, 101–102, 112–113
>   discussing pros and cons of fighting, 117–120
>   gossip, 38, 120–121
>   identifying peer abuse, 150
>   peer pressure and, 121
>   peer-instruction about bullying, 126–127
>   role of witnesses, 120–125
>   strategies for, 101–102
>   understanding psychology of bullies and victims, 108–109
>   *See also* adult intervention
peer mediation programs, 102, 125, 142–143, 151–150
peer violence. *See* bullying
Perry, David, 96, 97, 182
physical abuse, 13–29
>   from boyfriends, 19
>   as bullying, 10
>   examples of, 14–16
>   handguns and, 19–20, 29, 176
>   hazing and, 25–26, 29
>   horseplay versus, 13–14
>   witnesses to, 24
>   *See also* aggression *and* violence
Pipher, Mary, 26
popularity
>   of bullies, 108
>   and victims, 99
Porter, William, 162

power
>   and bullying, 9, 127, 183–184
>   using verbal abuse as, 31–32, 35–36
Power of Myth, The (Campbell and Moyers), 25–26
"Prime Time Live," 63
principals, 141
Project Essential curriculum, 165
Prothrow-Stith, Deborah, 117–120
provocative victims, 97, 102
psychological aspects
>   of bullies, 108–109
>   of victims, 109
Psychologically Battered Child, The (Garbarino, Guttmann, and Seeley), 45
put-downs, 38–39

racism and racial abuse, 123, 177
>   deterring, 203–205
Raphael, Lev, 113
reactive bullies, 102
Reavis, H. Kenton, 167–168
rejection, 47–48
religious harassment, 61
resources for bullying prevention, 189
Reviving Ophelia (Pipher), 26
Rhode, Ginger, 167–168
ritalin, 88
rites of passage, 25–27
rock music, 179
roles
>   locking children into, 76, 77
>   role playing, 149
Russo, Rene, 136–137

Safe School Report, 17
Sager, Nancy, 162
Sattel, Sue, 61–62
Sawyer, Diane, 63

school counselors, 142
schools
    authorities response to bullying, 16–17
    bullying prevention policies, 156–157, 185–186
    community service programs and, 126–127
    conflict–mediation and -resolution, 102, 125, 142–143
    crowding and aggression in, 24–25
    handguns and, 19–20, 29
    harassment and violence policies for, 66, 70, 195–201
    influences on bullying, 8, 103
    multicultural and gender–fair curriculum rule for, 203–205
    Peer Abuse Survey Form, 191–193
    prevalence of verbal abuse in, 39–42
    programs for bullying prevention, 160
    sexual harassment in, 68–69
    talking to principals of, 141
Schoolyard Bully Practicum (National School Safety Center), 181–182
SCRAPES, 159
Seamons, Brian, 51–52
Second Step curriculum, 166–167
Seeley, Janis, 45
self-blame, 132
self-esteem
    books about, 161
    building, 131
    clothing and, 121
Selman, Robert, 91, 182
sex education
    by adults, 153
    by peers, 64–65

sex education *(continued)*:
    sexual harassment and, 66, 70, 153
sexual abuse, 55–70
    adults' memories of, 11
    books about, 161
    contact, 58–60
    defining, 55–56
    gender and effect of, 60
    noncontact, 57–58
    peer, 62–69
    sexual harassment as, 61
    sexually abusive children, 63–64
    types of sexual activities, 56
    See also sexual harassment
sexual harassment
    educational programs about, 66, 70, 153
    flirting and, 67
    guidelines for, 61
    laws against, 153
    policies against, 61, 65, 195–201, 207
    in schools, 68–69
    verbal abuse as, 38
Sexual Harassment and Teens (Strauss and Espeland), 67
Sexual Harassment in Our Schools (Shoop and Hayhow), 69
sexual innuendo, 57
Sexual Respect Curriculum, The (Miner), 170
sexually abusive children, 63–64
Shanker, Albert, 66–67
Sheridan, Susan M., 168
Shoop, Robert, 69
Short-Camilli, Cam, 162
sibling abuse, 71–83
    adult intervention in, 74–76, 79–83
    adults' memories of, 11
    defining, 73
    frequency of, 73

siblings
    comparing, 76, 82
    negative feelings between, 74–76
Siblings Without Rivalry (Faber and Mazlish), 74
Sjostrom, Lisa, 162
Slaby, Ron, 182
social pressure to fight, 21–22, 133
spanking, 152–153
Spreading Kindness: A Program Guide (Kindness Campaign), 167
"Squash it!," 22–23
Stamenow, Dr. Stan, 162–163
Stein, Nan, 66, 162
Stephens, Ronald D., 183
Stick Up For Yourself! (Kaufman and Raphael), 113
STOP Violence Coalition, 164
storytelling, 133–134
Strauss, Susan, 67
suicides by teens, 100–101, 109
Surrey, Janet, 56

Tangney, June Price, 115
Task Force on Juvenile Sexual Offending, 55
Tattum, Delwyn, 182
teachers
    intervening with students, 143–147
    intervening with verbal abuse, 41–42
    response to bullying, 16–17
    violence against, 159–160
    watching for ostracization, 48–50, 53, 145–146
Teaching About Sexual Abuse (Huggins), 161
Teaching Cooperation Skills (Huggins), 161
Teaching Friendship Skills (Huggins), 161
teasing, 1–3
    distinguished from bullying, 12
    and Nathan Faris, 3–4
teenagers
    developmental changes of, 23
    hazing and, 25–26, 29
    homocide and, 22–23
    suicide and, 100–101, 109
television
    effect of sexual material on, 63
    violence and, 27–28, 29, 104, 178–179
Terr, Lenore, 176–177
terrorizing, 50–52
Titles VII and IX, Civil Rights Act (1964), 153
Tough Kid Book (Rhode, Jenson, and Reavis), 167–168
Tough Kid Social Skills Book (Sheridan), 168

unworthiness, 45

Vachss, Andrew, 45
Vanderwerff, Whitney, 180
verbal abuse, 31–43
    adults' memories of, 10–11
    as bullying, 10
    defining, 32–33, 42
    education about, 153
    emotional effects of, 37
    gossip, 38, 120–121
    intending harm, 33–35
    intensity and duration of, 35
    monitoring speech and, 42
    overpowering others with, 31–32, 35–36
    physical consequences of, 37–38
    prevalence in schools, 39–42
    put-downs and, 38–39

verbal abuse *(continued)*:
  recognizing, 153
  as sexual harassment, 38
  vulnerability of victims and,
    36–37
victims, 96–101
  ages, 10
  bullies as, 88
  consequences of being bullied,
    99–101
  creative responses to bullies,
    113
  disabled as, 34–35, 98–99,
    135–136
  of juvenile sexual offenders, 62
  kinds of, 96–97, 102, 113
  physical characteristics of, 98–99
  popular children as, 99
  qualities of, 97–98, 109, 152
  reinforcing role of, 77
  selected by bullies, 97–98
  self–blame and, 132
  strategies for thwarting bullies,
    101–102, 112–113
  teen suicides and, 100–101, 109
  vulnerability of, 10, 36–37
  witnesses and, 121–122, 124–
    125
video games, 179
violence
  against teachers, 159–160
  age factor and, 17–19, 21
  biological basis for, 24
  breakdown of families and,
    173–175
  bullies relationship to, 152
  fear of, 17–19
  increases in, 17
  prevention of bullying and,
    11–12

violence *(continued)*:
  pros and cons of fighting,
    117–120
  on television and in movies,
    27–28, 29, 104, 178–
    179
  See also aggression *and* physical
    abuse
violence prevention materials, 171
violent metaphors, 42
Von Oech, Roger, 147–148
vulnerability of victims, 10, 36–37

Walker, Lenore, 24
Welcome to the Dollhouse, 184
Whack on the Side of the Head, A (Von
  Oech), 147–148
What To Do When Kids Say "NO"
  (Behavior Intervention Support
  Team), 168–170
"When Children Abuse" (Cunningham and MacFarlane),
  62
Winsten, Jay, 19, 22–23
withholding relationship, 46
witnesses
  confronting bullies, 122–124
  participating in gossip, 120–121
  peer pressure and, 121
  to physical abuse, 24
  role of, 110–111
  sticking up for victims,
    121–122, 124–125
Woods, Melvin, 119

"You Carry The Cure In Your Own
  Heart" (Vachss), 45
youth gangs, 27